LIFE LESSONS *of a* DOBERMAN PINSCHER

SARAH C. BENOIT

LCMHC, LMHC

ISBN: 979-8-218-86679-2
ISBN: 979-8-218-86680-8

Cover and interior formatting by KUHN Design Group | kuhndesigngroup.com

For Remington

Thank you for reminding me what I am made of.

CONTENTS

INTRODUCTION

It is a beautiful early fall morning in New Hampshire. The leaves are starting to change because of the cooler nights, the sun is bright, and the air is crisp. Too cool for a skirt, so nice jeans will have to do for the office. I must be at work early today so our Doberman Pinscher puppy, Remington, will go to doggie daycare to spend his day before I come to get him.

Remington is excited about seeing everyone at doggy daycare. Sometimes when he is excited, he will pee. He is also seven months old and is starting to feel his hormones and has begun trying to mark his territory wherever we go. As we go into the lobby, Remington tries to pee on some toys and a display stand filled with soft-sided toys and treats for small dogs. I am just about to hand him off to the staff when I feel a warmth running down my leg that started at the knee. Remington has decided he needs to claim me as his own before I leave and proceeds to pee all over my leg. He is very proud afterward, while the doggie daycare staff laugh hysterically and try to assure me that this happens all the time. I am not so sure that this kind of thing happens all the time. My day is off to a stellar start, and now I need to rush back home and change my jeans and shoes before work begins.

This is just one example of my adventures with our Doberman Remington. I am guessing if you are reading this book and have a dog or know someone who does, you can probably relate on some level to the morning I had. Maybe you haven't had your puppy claim you through marking, but I am sure there are plenty of other examples out there that you look back on and either laugh or cry about while remembering.

Having had animals most of my life, adding another fur baby to our family felt like a natural next step, as my animals have provided immense comfort, plenty of laughter, and joy. Getting another dog didn't seem daunting; I was swept up in the thoughts of all the fun and excitement a puppy brings. Yet, the lessons I learned along the way from Remington were completely unexpected, as well as so powerful and transformative, that I felt I needed to share them with others in this book.

When we think about dogs, they are recognized for their unconditional love and support. Beyond unconditional love, dogs are wonderful teachers—they help us discover more about ourselves and if we let them, they guide us to love and support *ourselves* unconditionally.

By profession, I am a licensed psychotherapist so I spend my days listening to people's struggles, challenges, fears, and, hopefully, successes, as dogs can do as well. Sometimes I get to watch enormous growth in people, and that is such a reward. Throughout Remington's youth, I was challenged by many of the concepts people bring to me in most therapy sessions. I was living the concepts I talked about daily to others, in what felt like every moment of my personal life. Intellectually, I knew I was not alone in my puppyhood challenges and how that related to my daily life.

I was fortunate to have a husband, parents, and friends who

supported and validated me, and I wanted to be able to do the same for others. I want people to read this book and see that yes, the struggle is real, but it is also temporary with dogs. The life lessons are real and rewarding.

With over twenty years of experience in the field of psychology, I have had the privilege of collaborating with individuals from a diverse range of backgrounds and life circumstances. Through these experiences, one realization has consistently appeared: At our core, people are more alike than different. While the specifics of our lives—our stories, challenges, and circumstances—may differ, the lessons we draw from these experiences often share a universal similarity, which can also be experienced with our pets.

Another reason it was important for me to share my experience in this book is that I think a lot of people get Dobermans and give up on them too soon. When I look at the Doberman rescue pages, so many of them are between the ages of one and two. Their early years can be the most taxing, but if you can get through that period, you will have the best partner ever in your dog.

Life Lessons of a Doberman Pinscher is broken out into eleven sections. The first is a brief history of the Doberman Pincher breed to give you more of an idea of what dogs like Remington are all about. The following ten sections are segmented by each life lesson I wish to share but are not written about in order of importance.

- Lesson One: *You Can't Control Everything*

- Lesson Two: *Do What Works For You*

- Lesson Three: *Time Doesn't Stop*

- Lesson Four: *Patience*

- Lesson Five: *Perseverance*

- Lesson Six: *Be In It For The Long Haul*

- Lesson Seven: *You are Going to Fuck Up*

- Lesson Eight*: Confidence is Key*

- Lesson Nine: *You Don't Always Get What You Want*

- Lesson Ten: *Be Grateful and Have Fun*

Each section offers examples of how Remington and I navigated each life lesson: the good, bad, and the ugly.

In the end, Remington and I both learned a great deal. It may have been challenging, but it was a process I look back on and would not trade for the world. We both grew so much, and, in the end, I gained a loving companion who always has my back.

My hope is this book resonates with you, and you feel encouraged and empowered in approaching each new day with your furry companion.

Sarah and Sean Picking Remington Up From The Breeder

DOBERMAN HISTORY

The Doberman Pinscher is an often-misunderstood breed but is a special breed that deserves to be understood and appreciated. While this is not a comprehensive historical outline of the "Dobie," it gives a quick snapshot of the breed's origins and traits, and where people get these lovable dogs all wrong.

The Doberman Pinscher is a dominant, working breed that was first bred about 150 years ago in the 1880s; the American Kennel Club (AKC) recognized the Doberman as a dog breed in 1908. Most people know that the Doberman originates from Germany, but they do not necessarily know that it was a hated tax collector, by the name of Karl Friedrich Louis Dobermann, which was the original breeder of these dogs. Dobermann was a police officer and security guard also but believed he required the dog's protection when out collecting taxes from citizens. So, he set out to create the ideal guard dog.

In nineteenth-century Germany, Dobermans were trained as police dogs; it wasn't until I got our Dobermann puppy, Remington, and was doing more researching about that breed that I learned how large a role the Doberman played during World War II. Dobermans served in a variety of vital roles within the United States Marine Corps during World War II. They acted as scouts, alerting troops to hidden dangers and ambushes, and as sentries, guarding camps and defensive positions. Beyond these duties, they were trained to function as messengers, carry out search and rescue operations, and perform mine detection, making them indispensable partners on the battlefield. The majority of the 1st War Dog Platoon were Doberman Pinschers, with the remaining dogs being German Shepherds. (Ortiz, 2021)

The United States Marine Corps had what they called a war dog training program. At the inception, they secured sixty-two dogs, which they got from sources that included the United States Army, The Doberman Pinscher Club of America, Dogs for Defense, Inc., and individual owners. Dobermans weren't the only breed the Marines were interested in, but my focus here for this book is on the Doberman.

All dogs in the program had to be from 1 to 5 years old, weigh at least 50 pounds, and be 15 inches in height. Obviously, they could not be fearful or easily frightened. It is believed that the Marines favored the Doberman because they were able to adapt to heat due to their short hair. They were also good at doing scout and messenger work; scout work meant that they would detect mines or enemy troops. Messengers would follow their handlers and carry correspondence or supplies. The expectation was the use of the dogs "contributed directly to the killing of the enemy and keeping down casualties in units for which dogs were helping to supply security." (Putney, 2002)

The successes that war dogs had in World War II, specifically on D-Day, are impressive. Some examples include the following:

1. "On 'D' day, Andy, (a Doberman Pinscher) led 'M' Co. all the way to the roadblock. He alerted scattered sniper opposition and undoubtedly was the means of preventing loss of life" (Ortiz, 2021).

2. "Otto (a Doberman Pinscher) ... while working ahead of reconnaissance patrol alerted the position of a machine gun nest, and the patrol had time to take cover with no casualties when the machine gun began firing. Otto alerted the position at least one hundred yards away" (Ortiz, 2021).

3. A Doberman named Jack pointed out a sniper in a tree that was in a position to do a lot of harm; this allowed the US Marine to eliminate the sniper (Ortiz, 2021).

4. Another Doberman named Rex alerted his handlers to Japanese soldiers in the area that were planning a morning attack. Due to Rex's notification, their Marines were not surprised (Ortiz, 2021).

The Doberman's service to their country is honorable and was lifesaving.

Today, most people think all Dobermans are the same; however, there are actually two types of Dobermans: the American and European Doberman. You may have noticed that sometimes I am using Doberman spelled with one "n" and sometimes I am spelling Dobermann with two "ns." The American Doberman is spelled with the single "n" and, when talking in general terms, the single "n" Doberman is widely accepted. When referencing the European Dobermann, many spell with the double "n."

European Dobermanns, in particular, are very muscular, strong, and have remarkably high stamina and exercise requirements (Doberman Planet, 2024). My Doberman Remington is of European descent; both of his parents are European and are large, beautiful dogs with a healthy lineage of longevity.

The American Doberman is elegant, sleek in appearance, with a narrower chest and thinner legs: they are also what you would typically see in American AKC dog shows. The European Dobermanns have a broader head, a broader chest, and compact, muscular bodies. At 8 weeks, Remington weighed 20 pounds and now at the time of this writing, at one year, he is 100 pounds. His brother, Roman, is 110 pounds. They are big boys.

Both versions of the breed also have some temperament differences. The American Doberman tends to be less assertive and have slightly less energy than the European Dobermann, but that is not to say that they are lazy or lacking in the protective arena. The European Dobermann oozes alertness and strength, having an intense work ethic and drive. They can also be stubborn, so it is important they have a strong leader in their owner who offers consistent training and positive reinforcement that is balanced with the appropriate level of correction.

I think it is also worth mentioning that Dobermans make excellent service dogs, which are dogs trained to perform specific tasks for someone with a disability. They are not the first breed that comes to mind for people when they think of service dogs, but they really are a great fit for the role. Dobermanns are highly intelligent, learn quickly, love to "work," and are vastly focused on their person. While I was in Denver last summer for a conference, one of the attendees had a Doberman service dog; she was an American Doberman, so she was a bit smaller in stature. It was amazing to see her in action, as she was extremely focused on her owner and exuded a calm, reassuring presence. You could tell she was both scanning the environment and making sure her person was okay.

YOU CAN'T CONTROL EVERYTHING

A puppy is a lot of work to care for, especially an eight-week-old puppy. When you take the puppy home, remember he (or she) is in an unfamiliar place with unfamiliar people and animals. He is excited but scared. Curious but cautious. Your puppy has a new bed, new toys, new everything. You think, *Okay, we have got all our bases covered. He has when he needs, and we know how to do this.* Well, I could not have been more wrong.

The first two weeks that my husband, Sean and I, had our dog Rowdy, I cried every day. (Rowdy is our thirteen-year-old mixed breed rescue dog from Tennessee.) He was the first puppy we had cared for as adults, and we experienced a lot. It was going to be different with our new Doberman puppy, Remington, as I thought to myself, *I have done this before. This won't be so bad. Remington likes the crate; Rowdy hated it. Potty training with Rowdy was easy, so Remington will be easy too. Getting up every hour and a half is tough but again, I've got this. I've done this before.*

Well, that first week with Remington yielded no sleep. Remington actually did pretty well in his crate and slept through the night. The part that took me by surprise was not just the adjustment of Remington to the family, but the other three animals (our dog Rowdy, our Maine Coon Lucy, and our orange rescue cat Charlie) and us adjusting to Remington. Remington was full of energy. Those little razor-sharp teeth hurt because he didn't know the difference between his plush toy, the kitten, and our feet: I did not remember Rowdy being as mouthy and aggressive. Combine Remington's energy, constant mouthing, and biting, along with how high maintenance he was, and my stress levels shot right up.

He had his first vet appointment during that first week of being home with us from the breeder. At that time, I was not even making sense at the vet and almost passed out due to stress over this dog, which I never experienced before. My anxiety was at Mach 4 while my logical brain was taking a break. The most poignant moment at the vet, besides the rundown of numerous vaccines Remington had to get, foods to eat and avoid, and where to not go because of his age-related immunity, was our conversation about neutering. The breeder had told me that it was not advised to neuter before one year; that is the one thing that stuck in my brain from our conversations.

So, when the vet said, "Being that he is a large breed, we don't recommend neutering prior to a year," I don't know what I heard, but my guard went up. Immediately, I replied, "Well, we are really set on not neutering him until at least twelve months." The vet looked at me with a blank stare. After a few seconds, I realized what I said, essentially the exact same thing as the vet, and apologized for my lack of sleep and comprehension. Reflecting on that conversation at the vet could have been my first clue about what was happening in my head. I was so fixated on "doing this thing right" with Remington that I was already losing sight of the forest among the trees.

I had waited so long to have a Doberman of my own. I revere the breed and wanted to do right by our Doberman, but I also had looked back at the mistakes we had made with Rowdy and didn't want to repeat those again. Sean and I had talked at length about things we didn't do with regards to training, socialization and the like, that we wanted to do differently with Remington. This was especially important to us because Remington is a bigger dog, and his mere appearance can be intimidating to others.

Remington's time both in and out of the crate, bathroom breaks, as well as mealtimes, was actually printed out on paper. What I was feeding him (kibble, raw eggs, coconut oil, probiotics, ground turkey or beef) and how much was measured out. (Wow, even reading this, I sound neurotic.) This regimen extended to the rest of us in the family. If Remington was in the crate, that meant I needed to take care of everything possible: dishes, laundry, dinner, client emails and phone calls, feeding myself, taking a shower. How did I manage everything before this dog? If everything did not get done, I was primed for a meltdown.

This is where my profession kicks in. I am a psychotherapist, not a psycho-therapist, which some of those close to me might argue. I meet people every day who have anxiety, and we work together to help them manage it. I offer suggested strategies and techniques, such as using logic, deep breathing and box breathing. (Box breathing is when you breathe in for a count of 4, hold for a count of 4, and slowly exhale for a count of 4), and grounding. I also use EMDR (Eye Movement Desensitization and Reprocessing) and CBT (Cognitive Behavioral Therapy) with my clients.

However, I was not using any of these techniques on myself. I needed to take a page from my clients and do the work I encourage and support them in doing in order to feel better myself. First, I needed to calm my nervous system down, then I needed to figure out where all of this anxiety was coming from. I have always struggled with anxiety, but this anxiety felt very different and was more intense than I had experienced previously. Obviously having a puppy was challenging but that couldn't be the entire reason for my anxiousness. I was not ready, however, to get to the root of the problem. To start, I needed to exist but, in a calm, grounded manner.

What helps me feel grounded and calm is routine and structure. I have always needed to know what is coming next; I need predictability. So, I put Remington on a schedule as I have my clients on a schedule and know which days I work in the office and which days I work remotely (thus being at home with Remington). It was time to take my job as a puppy parent seriously, so I needed to get him into training. He was nine weeks old, so it was time to get moving and get a jump on him becoming a well-trained dog. I started calling trainers, as I wanted someone local and who knew Dobermans. I started making phone calls, but the overwhelming messages from trainers were that classes were full, it was too soon to train, and "you just need to enjoy this time with your puppy and bond." Oh, and by the way, make sure you socialize your puppy.

That was another thing I had to do so I printed out fifty things to expose Remington to in order to help him be a well-socialized puppy. I covered the gamut: loud noises, heavy equipment, different surfaces under his feet, different smells, and textures. Different people: people in uniform, people with hoods and sunglasses on. Riding in the car. Riding in the truck. Riding in the boat. Teaching him to put his paws in water and swimming.

I took Remington to Tractor Supply for a field trip, and he had a wonderful time. Met a few people. Met another dog. Peed on the post in the store. Great puppy adventure. Two days later, he had snot an inch long running out of his nose and started to cough. I took pictures to show the vet the size of his nasal discharge in case no one believed me. We got to the vet, but I was not allowed to walk him in and had to carry him into a sanitized room where the tech and vet were gloved, gowned, and masked. They were not saying kennel cough, but an upper respiratory infection for which he needed antibiotics. They asked if he had been near other dogs recently, then told me he couldn't be around dogs that we did not know their histories and where they had been. We couldn't go for walks on the road in case of other dogs having been there, and ninety percent of my neighbors had dogs. We were also told to NOT take him to stores unless I carried him in and put him in a shopping cart. I am sorry but I am NOT putting my Doberman in a shopping cart, but I should have.

I left the vet feeling horrible and confused. I called back the next day and said, "You've told me what I cannot do, which is a lengthy list. What exactly can I do then to socialize my puppy?" They had to confer with the technician and call me back. To this day, I cannot remember what they said to me. I just remember feeling frustrated and confused on what I was to do. The window to optimal puppy socialization was shrinking; I was on a mission, and things were getting in the way of completing that mission. This infection also set back Remington's vaccination schedule by two weeks. I needed his rabies shot to finally start training classes in June, and I "couldn't" wait again to start training so we could get a handle on him.

Oh, the could'ves, would'ves, and should'ves. Why couldn't I wait? Anxiety is why. I was wasting time waiting. Mind you, I really had started some training on my own. We were working on potty training and sitting while we waited. I was exposing Remington to what I could when I could, and my husband was taking him to work two days a week, so Remington got, and continues to get, a lot of exposure at the country club. (My husband is the superintendent at a country club.)

Is anyone noticing a theme here? Maybe a theme of control and, better yet, perfectionism?

Remember earlier I talked about calming my anxiety and getting to the root of it. Again, at this point on this journey, I am nowhere close to finding the root cause of my anxiety, again aside from the obvious stresses of having a puppy. But why was this puppy causing so much anxiety for me? Why did this journey feel so big and challenging? By now, I was chalking it up to him being young and me not having done this, training a dog, in twelve years.

I am also chalking it up to his breed. Both American and European Dobermans are highly in tuned with their human emotions. That point right there always sticks in my head because I know that when I am unsettled, frustrated, anxious, or whatever, I am transferring those feelings right down the leash to my dog. Hence why I wanted to be doing everything "right" to avoid this.

In hindsight, I think another contributing factor to my anxiety is that I was in the middle of menopause; this is another issue I discuss with clients at length. It never occurred to me that the intensity of my anxiety and my overwhelming need to control could be related to my own body and the changes it was going through. I surely could not control my hormones, but I could control all the aspects of raising a puppy. Or so I thought.

When we try and control everything, we deplete ourselves rather quickly, depleting our energy, both mentally and physically, and we do not set ourselves up for success. For some, it is an easy trap to fall into but one that is not worth it. If you give yourself permission to let go and not obsess over the little things, the big things really do work out in the end.

Lesson One: You Can't Control Everything.

Remington's First Boat Ride

Remington's First Boat Ride

LESSON TWO

DO WHAT WORKS FOR YOU

Back to the idea of training Remington, while dealing with anxiety, I finally had gotten a training class to fall into place for Remington a short time later after starting to look. The class was once a week for six weeks and was basically puppy kindergarten. I was excited to start and get him on a path to success. The trainer bred Dobermans and owned a business that offered training, boarding, and daycare, so I figured this was going to be perfect. The first session was supposed to be an orientation where we brought our paperwork and our dog; it turned out it was a small class with only three dogs, including Remington. One owner didn't have her dog because she didn't think she was supposed to. The other owner brought her dog, and he was fairly small, so not a Doberman.

We weren't off to a great start when the instructor wasn't there yet; it seemed that she was running a bit late, and the owner who didn't bring her dog suggested I leave mine in the car for this session. Based on her interactions once we were inside the building for orientation, and she realized what breed Remington was, I believe she was scared by my dog. She later said her dog was going to be fearful of my dog when classes began. (We chose not to crop his ears, which lends a less intimidating look in my opinion of Dobermans. We are not opposed to the practice but for our home and lifestyle, it didn't make sense to add ear-cropping to our plate right off the bat. You also have a short window in which to do it, and many vets will not do it.)

Unfortunately, Remington was a lot to manage in that first class. He took a big poop on the floor because he was so excited and nervous. When the trainer noticed, I got the first lecture about the firmness of his poop and what I should be feeding him. I was open to the feedback at the time and went home and changed immediately from pumpkin to sweet potato. (It made no difference by the way.) It was also recommended by the trainer that I start using a slip lead on him so he would stop pulling, and I would have more control, so I was happy to purchase said slip lead and started using it the next day. The trainer then told me to go home and play with my dog, make him run for about a half-hour to get his excess energy out. At that point, Remington was three months old.

I started using the slip lead immediately, but all he would do was choke himself. Commanding Remington to stop pulling, which was part of the training, was not doing anything either. Well, it was doing something: it was helping me feel like a failure, inept, and out of control. But I was stuck with the feelings for now. During the following weeks of sessions, Remington was pulling all over the place, trying to get to the other two dogs. The trainer took him from me at one point and basically dragged him into submission. It was hard to watch, and I didn't know how I was feeling about it. Yet, I knew my feelings were written all over my face, and then I started to tear up; more reinforcement that I was doing everything wrong.

At one point, the trainer asked how much Remington weighed (fifty pounds at the time) but thought he was six months old; I reminded her he was only three months old. She then told me I was going to have a tough time with him and that I was too sensitive in training him. This was not the first time she would say this to me during the sessions. Again, tears were starting to well up in my eyes, and I was questioning if I could do it. If I even should be doing this. Should I be a puppy parent? Was I strong enough to do this? I cried the whole way home and asked my husband to come to classes with me for support. The trainer wanted me to do the training, but I wanted Sean there.

After that second training session with Remington, I started to get truly angry. I knew that I was a sensitive person, even an empath, but I did not like being told that it was a detriment and in front of the other class members. I work with people every day and reassure them that having feelings and emotions is okay. It's okay to be sensitive and be yourself, but here I was being told that it wasn't, and I had to stop being me. Thankfully, I was able to turn that anger into resolve, as I was not giving up on this puppy, training, or myself.

I was extremely fortunate to have had a friend who had two Dobermans, and she had been a lifeline and lifesaver for me throughout this puppy process with Remington. She also helped become my voice of reason many times throughout this journey. I explained the pulling problem with the slip lead, and she offered me the leash her dog used when she was a young puppy. It was similar to a gentle lead and had a part that went over the nose, which sits on a pressure point and prevents the dog from pulling. This leash was a Godsend, and the following week, I walked into training with a new dog. The trainer noticed; ironically, she never heard of this type of leash, but she was impressed at how well Remington did when we used it.

I basically explained that the slip lead did not work for him, and I had to find something else. I also shared that I fully expected to use a prong collar when he was old enough to keep him under control. The trainer agreed but also went on to say that people would probably give me a hard time because of it. I might get looks, but I could cover it up with a bandanna so that people wouldn't see it; that was often what she did with her dogs.

I was, and am still, comfortable with people disagreeing on how I raise my dog, train my dog, feed my dog, and what tools I employ to control my dog. I am not going to lie though; everyone does have their opinion, and they think that you want to hear it. Sometimes I do and I welcome it; other times, not so much. However, I don't feel that any of us should have to hide or defend our choices. I think it is important to make decisions based on what works best for you, your dog, and your situation.

This is one of the themes/situations I often see in my work with clients. People get a lot of advice from others. Some they want and solicit, and other advice is completely unwanted and unsolicited. I always tell people at the end of the day you must do what works best for you. You have to be able to sleep at night with the decisions you have made. People can offer up whatever they want, but you only have to take what you want of advice.

Overall, training for Remington was getting better, but I still dreaded that one training day each week. The expectations for training Remington at home were 20 to 30 minutes each day and all at one time, going over what we learned in sessions. The trainer's reasoning was that "he could handle it" each day. I was diligent about that, as well as walking him daily for the recommended duration for his age. What I didn't know until later was that I was burning my dog out, as well as myself, in reinforcing all this training.

The last few weeks of training got dragged out because of the trainer canceling or forgetting about class. Because of the last class being missed by the trainer and then rescheduled at the last minute, Remington never graduated from kindergarten. But little did he realize that later, he would go from essentially a community college to the Ivy Leagues of dog training. More on that later.

During this time of training and puppyhood, Remington was also starting to have some skin issues, such as bumps and growths. As I mentioned earlier, in my need for control, I was diligent about Remington's diet. I followed what the breeder recommended at the start and then switched everything up after listening to the veterinarian. The vet was concerned about the high fat in the beef I was feeding Remington, so I switched him to turkey. He was also concerned about the raw egg he got daily; most vets believe raw food can make your dog sick and do not support raw food in diets. So, they wanted Remington on a large breed puppy kibble and at six months, they wanted us to incorporate adult kibble, so he didn't grow faster than he was already growing. Because I took every recommendation to heart, I can't tell you how many hundreds of dollars I spent on bags of dog food, only to end up having to donate them all in the end.

Part of the reason for the food problems was because with these skin issues, many questions came; it was a particularly challenging time for all of us. As I mentioned, Remington had bumps and developed growths, which no one was quite sure of. He was very itchy and dry. We spent a lot of time between the regular vet and the emergency vet but were not getting far at all with relief. It got to the point that the regular vet wanted us not only on an elimination diet, but also prescription food. With the elimination diet, we even had to change up the heartworm and flea and tick prevention medicine because they contained beef, and the vet wasn't sure if he was allergic to beef. Let me tell you, beef is in everything, even salmon-based food. It got to the point that the only thing we could feed Remington was the prescription hydrolyzed food. No treats, no additional anything.

Without any real change, the vet was stumped and was going to surgically remove Remington's growths, since they weren't going away. However, in the span of a weekend, he went from having four to eight growths. I sent pictures to my friend with the two Dobermans. She said they looked like warts to her, and when she was a kid, her mom used to put Vitamin E on her warts so they went away. What did I have to lose, right? Well, low and behold, it worked! I was so relieved. To this day, I don't know if they were officially warts but if he gets bumps or growths like that, I immediately go get the Vitamin E.

During this time, we also secured an appointment with an animal dermatologist. The wait was a couple of months to see them, but we didn't know what else to do and felt like we hit a wall. Remington wasn't feeling well obviously, and it came out in his behavior and tolerance, or lack thereof; that behavior easily translated to me. Again, there was that anxiety and feelings of helplessness and frustration. I didn't feel that the prescription food was the answer, but we agreed to follow it through until the end.

Because Remington was uncomfortable and grumpy, and we couldn't use training treats, we had to get creative with his training. This dog's best friend, with the exception of our neighbor's dog Maverick, was his frisbee. Nothing trumped the frisbee. In order to work on sit, down, and stay, especially with distractions outside, the frisbee was the answer. However, being a puppy, Remington hadn't learned the concept of manners and personal space. Personal space is a tough one for Dobermans because they are the quintessential Velcro dogs. During playtime, he was notorious for running into me, and my legs were covered in bruises from our collisions. Not something that was easy to explain. Even my dermatologist noted it, and I had to explain I had a puppy and that he was large and powerful. Teaching him proper play manners was a necessity.

Going back to the food issue, we agreed to keep Remington on the prescription food for the full twelve-week recommendation. The day that the dermatologist agreed we could take him off the food, we were so excited. But now we had another decision to make: What were we going to feed him? Kibble—if so, what brand and what type? Raw—how much of a hard time were we going to get for doing that? We also had to really do our homework because there was raw food, but not all were complete in minerals, nutrients, and vitamins. Time for my Type A personality to kick in again. I researched and compared so many brands of raw food.

You also have to factor in raw, freeze dried, tubes, chunks, or patties of meat. What size, 1-pound, 2-pound or 5-pounds? Do we have the storage space for what we would need, given his feeding need? I wasn't as comprehensive on the kibble end, as I knew what brands we were comfortable with and what worked for our other animals.

Shortly after our first training experience, we started working with a new trainer. He was very educated in all things dogs and had a lot of great suggestions around the raw food concept. He was pro-raw for many reasons, one of which was the success he had seen with his own dogs and allergies. We went back and forth with the idea, and I spent so much time focusing on this situation that I actually started dreaming about dog food and what we were going to do. I wasn't stressed out at all about this decision, but I was!

Where we landed was a diet consisting of half-raw food and

half-kibble, along with his supplements of salmon oil, Vitamin E, probiotics, and things like sardines and other goodies to mix things up.

The amount of effort we put into this food issue seemed extensive, but the amount of effort we were putting into this puppy seemed more extensive. That said, the effort looked to be working for us and was paying off for Remington. Having a plan and being able to put it into action helped reduce my anxiety and enabled me to relax as well. As I mentioned previously, our emotions translate directly down that leash to our dog. I think Remington noticed I was more relaxed too after this was settled; at least, I like to think that was the case.

After all the training, food research, and feedback from the trainers, vets, and friends, I ultimately took and implemented the parts that worked for our dog and our family. Everyone had their opinions and suggestions, and I was able to parse out the things I was most comfortable with and what seemed to work best for Remington to move us forward again.

Lesson Two: Do What Works for You

Rowdy Showing Remington How a Good Sit is Done

LESSON THREE

TIME DOES NOT STOP

At the end of the last chapter, I made the bold statement that having a plan and putting it into action made me feel more relaxed with my puppy Remington. It is true that having Remington's food struggle figured out made me feel more relaxed, but let's talk about this on broader terms. I was still not relaxed at all with raising our puppy.

All I wanted was for things to slow down and to catch my breath. When working with clients that are grieving the death of a loved one, they often want life to slow down. They sometimes want to go back in time when their loved one was still there, and the grief was non-existent. They also realize that their life is now vastly different; their world has changed, yet everyone around them continues to move on. They are not ready to move forward and haven't reached the point where there is acceptance of their new reality. This is where I was in Remington's puppy journey.

To clarify, let's go back in time a bit. My husband Sean and I had thought it would be good for Remington to go to doggy daycare to help him socialize. He had been a few times when we worked with the original trainer, and I will admit while he seemed to like it, it felt a bit chaotic and drove my anxiety through the roof. For example, pick-up time for Remington felt crazy and unhinged. There were dogs barking, so your dog was excited to see you but was distracted by the other dogs. From there, you had to harness them up while they were wiggling around and wouldn't sit still, and then you had to get them out the door into the car to then harness them again in to get safely home.

We changed from that doggy daycare and went to another doggie daycare. We were happier and more comfortable with the new establishment on many levels. Remington made friends and had new experiences that were more worthwhile. Looking back, there were so many things I did not know and did not recognize about doggy daycares. The most important thing that I could piece together was that the daycare activities were aggravating Remington's skin, and aggravated skin made him very unsettled and grumpy. I had also been discouraged from sending him to daycare because much like dog parks, there are two types of dogs: those that get bullied and those that are bullies. Also, any training you are working on with your trainer at home can get undone because daycare may use different commands, hand signals, and techniques.

Remington would come home and be partially exhausted but partially amped up. Again, I really didn't think much of it. Everyone loved him, but at the same time, we were getting reports that he knocked an employee/volunteer over. Some of the younger staff were intimidated by him; he was a wild maniac and wouldn't listen, bounding out of his crate with wild abandon. He nipped someone in the butt and tried humping a female puppy the same age, and they had to be separated. The list went on. Then we got the call that he went after another male dog, and we had to pick him up. He was no longer welcome, but we could try again in about a month after he was neutered.

The day that call came, I was just about to start a full day of clients, and my husband was on his way to a funeral. Thankfully, my husband was still local and was able to pick Remington up and bring him home. You get a call like that, and all sorts of things can come up. I felt ashamed and defeated, like I wasn't doing a respectable job in my training of Remington. I technically "knew" that I couldn't control his behavior at daycare, but I felt like I should have somehow trained him better and could have done more.

The expulsion from daycare also threw a big monkey wrench into our plans. Four weeks from then, we were going to go on vacation. We never had a honeymoon so we figured we would do that for our ten-year anniversary. Everything was paid for, and we had been looking forward to the trip. Remington was supposed to board at the same place he went to daycare; that was not a possibility now. So, I had to find a place that would take him that was reputable, safe, and had availability.

Time to scramble. I looked online, asked our trainer, asked neighbors and friends. My friend Erin, the one with the two Dobermans, came through again. She told me about the place she used, and the fact that your dog did not have to be with other dogs was appealing. They have their own space, had play time with staff, had enrichment opportunities if you wanted them, and there was someone on staff twenty-four hours a day. The only drawback was that the facility was an hour from our house.

A new place to board also meant getting all of Remington's medical vaccines and documentation to the facility. Even though I knew he had everything he needed, he also had to have a window of time that he hadn't been to another facility, which included the vet, the groomer, a pet store, or a doggie daycare. After I looked at his appointments, he was going to be cutting it close, but he would be fine. They approved of his stay, and there was a sense of relief for us.

Again, that relief was short-lived. Once again, I started to feel that I just wanted things to slow down so I could catch my breath. This was the same time Remington was starting to get those growths, and he had an exceptionally large one on the back of his neck. The vet prescribed antibiotics, and he was on the tail-end of them during his stay at the boarding facility. He was also on the prescription food, so I had to bag and label two meals for each day, as well as make sure his medication was labeled and spelled out appropriately.

Next hurdle, who could be Remington's emergency contact? This was required and with him, the biggest issue was who could manage him in the event of an emergency while we were gone. He was large, strong, and still kind of wild. Fortunately, my friend Erin offered, and I took her up on that. One of my husband's colleagues offered as well so we had two, and they were both fairly close to the boarding facility.

One of my biggest fears was that something was going to happen to Remington, and we would have to come back from our trip early. Life with Remington had been so unpredictable and fast-paced up until this point, so why would things be any different now?

We got everyone settled: Remington at boarding, Rowdy at Gram Camp. (My husband's parents take Rowdy to their house and come over twice a day to feed the cats and take care of the chickens.) We were packed and ready to go, looking forward to time away and a good night's sleep.

It was strange being away for more than a weekend, but it was much needed. I really needed things to slow down, and it felt easy settling into our resort and looking forward to doing fun things. I was worried about Remington but believed he would be ok.

One day, we were eating lunch at a restaurant down the street from our resort. We were sitting by the water, enjoying local cuisine and cocktails. Suddenly, my phone started to ring, and it was Erin (Remington's emergency contact). A wave of sheer panic came over me, and I just looked at my husband and said, "It's Erin." I answered the phone and didn't even say hello, just simply said, "What's wrong?" Remington had soft stools, and the boarding facility wanted to know if it was okay to give him pumpkin, since he was on a restricted diet. Erin figured it was okay but wanted to make sure. What a relief that, that was all it was.

In that split second before I answered, we were sure we would have to cancel the rest of our vacation and book a flight home. Erin felt terrible for calling too because she knew it freaked me out. It took a minute to ground myself again after the phone call and put myself back in vacation mode. But soft poop was not a big deal, and I was happy the boarding facility was paying attention. I was also grateful that Erin was there to help.

The rest of our vacation was relaxing, fun, and uneventful, with no news from home. However, the day before we left, the anxiety kicked in again for me. I knew I was headed back to getting up super early, with a velociraptor of a puppy and a busy week of clients ahead. We even had to cut our stay short by one day because the airline changed our departing flight, which meant we needed to get back to the airport location the night before due to the early flight.

Getting home was seamless and smooth. What a relief we could get home, make dinner, and just settle in. Rowdy had been dropped off a couple of hours before we got home, and we were picking Remington up in the morning. We were excited to see Rowdy as he greeted us in the mudroom. Then we walked into the kitchen. There were two huge piles of vomit, which we knew were not from the cats. Then we went upstairs. Holy hell! Cat diarrhea in three rooms. That thought of easing back home was squashed, as it took two hours to clean everything up. Everyone in the house was put on probiotics and zero treats for a couple of days.

The next morning, we picked Remington up and brought him home. We worried he may have forgotten who we were after being gone for a week, but he did not and was extremely excited to see us and go home. Unfortunately, his skin was so dry and flaky. He was also super itchy, and the biggest bump on his neck, which was just shy of the size of a nickel, crusted over and was starting to lift off.

I felt like it never stopped. Yes, we had a reprieve for a week, but nothing was stopping at home. There was no break for Remington and his skin issues, and we still had six weeks to wait for the dermatologist. It felt like the hits kept coming, but we also had to hurry up and wait.

About six weeks prior to our trip, I started to rethink my anxiety in terms of what I would tell my patients. Medication is a last resort for me, personally and professionally, but I had to put that option back on the table. Part of my practice included psychedelic integration, and I had taken microdosed psilocybin over the spring into summer. Admittedly, I was not doing a decent job setting my daily intention and reflection, still too frazzled to slow down and take the time to be present with myself. When I did, I really half-assed it. I think I wanted the medicine to do the work for me, which was not how it even worked. The worst part was that I knew this.

I had been on an antidepressant since my mid- to late-twenties. I got off it about a year and a half before we got Remington and was successful in staying off of it, as I felt great without it. I could also drink grapefruit juice again. What a bonus. (Unfortunately, grapefruit juice interfered with the medication I was taking and altered its effectiveness.) But as of late, my anxiety had grown to the point of near-panic attacks regularly and a lot of tears. I decided to go back on my antidepressant but at the lowest dose possible.

Overall, it helped, but along with feeling better came this dilemma. Here I helped people process and integrate their psychedelic journeys, and I used pharmaceuticals. I was conflicted and felt like a fraud. For the longest time, I did not believe that pharmaceuticals were the answer for me, as well as for many people. Yes, they do have their place, but the bigger problem is we get complacent and just stay on them instead of trying to get off them. We don't test them to see if we really need them, and most doctors don't encourage that line of thinking. So, here I was purposely going back on them. My prescriber even told me that if I needed to up the dose, that wouldn't be a problem and to just let her know. My stint back on antidepressants was short-lived; I think the medicine helped a little bit, but they didn't solve the problem, and I wasn't willing to up the dose.

Just the other day, I told a client that just because the world is going ninety miles per hour, it doesn't mean we can't take time out to regroup, ground ourselves, and gather our thoughts. It is okay to pull over in the breakdown lane until you feel it is safe to drive again. Not one time during this stint with Remington had I been able to truly adopt that mantra. I have tried, and I have maybe slowed down to seventy-five miles per hour, but I never stopped in the breakdown lane. I think for me, there is a fear of stopping; if I stop, I may not start again. The reality is that that thinking is totally irrational; I have to start again, and I will start again. I think the fear is also if I slow down too much, how hard it will be to catch up. That's assuming I have to catch up to my current pace in life. Sometimes the construction areas we conjure up in our minds are worse than reality.

It is okay that time doesn't stop; it just means we may need to adjust our perspective.

Lesson Three: Time Does Not Stop

Remington's First Birthday

PATIENCE

P atience has never been one of my strong suits. Colleagues used to make fun of me early in my psychotherapy career, reminding me that "It is not about the product, Sarah, but the process." My response was often, "Fuck the process." Yes, those words were uttered by a therapist. I fully acknowledge that I am not a good patient and can even be a difficult one at best. However, even I must admit the process has value.

Seeing the value in Remington's skin struggles continued to be part of my process and his as well. All of the hurry-up and wait business started to become arduous. I also was getting frustrated regarding his training, as I felt like I was trying so hard to get him to be a good boy and be able to follow through on the commands he was learning. He was smart so why was he having such a tough time doing what he was told? Why was he chasing the cat and growling at him? Why was he nipping at me the more I worked with him? He was, and is, a good boy, but I had to acknowledge that he was struggling. Remington didn't feel well, and it would come out in numerous ways. Shit, I was struggling, and I didn't feel well.

After some honest and emotional conversations with our new trainer, Ian, I was reminded of my own Type A personality and the fact that I was burning out my dog and myself. My mother had given me similar feedback in that I wasn't going to be able to do things perfectly, and I needed to give myself a break.

One of the last things I wanted to do was make our puppy's life even more challenging. I wished he could talk and tell me what it felt like to be in his itchy, bumpy skin. But I am a person therapist, not an animal therapist. There are some flaws with my thinking here though, as I was only thinking about Remington: I was not thinking about myself, my husband, and the other animals. Those other factors were not completely off the table, but they certainly did not play an equal part in my life.

Some of those emotional moments in training ended up having some significant takeaways. For example, part of me was still in the mentality of our first trainer, which was all about product: it was all about the perfect sit, down, stay, and come. If Remington did the command, great, time to move on to the next one. Check the box and move on to the next level. There was no process going on in my head. I wanted results, wanted him to know his commands like our older dog Rowdy. Hmmm, expecting a puppy to act like an older dog? How unrealistic was that? I also seemed to be forgetting that a twelve-and-a-half-year-old dog had a lot of repetition in his repertoire more than a young puppy.

In hindsight, Ian was teaching us important lessons and integrating Remington into our family. We were being taught and reminded how to be the leaders of our pack, and we were teaching Remington his place in the pack. My soft spot for animals did not necessarily always come in handy. It was easy for me and important to have empathy in therapy sessions. However, it got me into trouble in teaching my Dobermann that I was in charge, not him.

My patience was poor, especially in the beginning. Like I said, I wanted Remington to do what he was supposed to do. I also wanted the other animals in our home to not provoke or get frustrated with Remington. They were adding variables that I knew if they were not there, it would make my like easier. That being said, I also would not trade any of them. I won't lie; on one really difficult day, I did tell the animals I was going to give them all away, except for our Maine Coon cat Lucy. I would not really do that, but it just goes to show we say things out of frustration that we really don't mean, even with animals.

For me, patience is also a good reminder about slowing down, chunking things down even. I believe in the power of breaking things down to the point of manageability and keeping it simple. When we feel overwhelmed, it is not easy to be patient or even feel sane sometimes. When tasks, projects, or interactions are whittled down into smaller tidbits, it is easier to keep moving forward, and we feel more successful in doing this. Think of it like building a foundation. You start to see things come together and click when things fit with one another; that is actually a rewarding feeling.

If all we are doing is focusing on what isn't working, or the fact that we are not there yet, things feel even more challenging, and the emotional fuse can get noticeably short. Even as we speak, or as I write, my fuse is short with Remington right now. I am sitting here trying to write, and he is getting into an argument with his crate door. Yet, it helps to reframe how you are thinking about a situation. I could sit here and get really angry because Remington barking at his crate is annoying, or I can choose to laugh about it and wonder what kind of conversation he thinks he is having with that door. Obviously, it may not be easy to engage in the latter frame of mind, but it's worth a try. Also, the more you try, the more likely you are to succeed.

Yesterday was a good example of the power of reframing. My day was summed up by me writing, "Patience is being pulled onto the ground, into a stone wall, having my lunch toppled over onto the table before I could even take a bite and getting body-slammed while playing frisbee." In short, that summed up my morning, afternoon, and evening with Remington. I was not happy after being pulled down into a stone wall and came out with scrapes and bruises. However, when it came down to telling my husband about it, I had to laugh because when Remington realized he had pulled me down (why I didn't let go is beyond me, as I have let go over less), he stopped, turned around, and just looked at me, as if to say, "Momma, what are you doing sitting on the ground?" When he pulled my glove off the table, which then led to my lunch bowl literally flipping over onto the table and rendering my food all over the place, which Rowdy took advantage of as a free meal, I could have gotten angry and yelled at Remington. Instead, I just cleaned it up and made something else. Same with the hip check when playing frisbee. Remington didn't run into me on purpose; we happened to move sideways at the same time and in the same direction. At the end of the day, I just had to laugh about it. He's a puppy, and if I just stay angry or frustrated at him, it only exhausts me while he has long forgotten about it.

There is some humility that is necessary with patience as well, going back to when I talked about control and perfectionism—neither are realistic. Identifying why you are so impatient is an important part of the process or moment. For me, it, more often than not, comes back to the need or want to be in control. The more things I can control, the less I believe my anxiety to be. But I can't control everything, and I certainly cannot control a puppy. He has to be allowed to be himself and figure things out, and that is where the patience part comes in. Remington isn't just going to do things or not do things because it is what I want. This is especially true if he hasn't learned certain manners or skills.

This understanding seems to help by reminding myself of the purpose. For example, what is the purpose of our adventure outside? Is it to play or train? What are my intentions or expectations? Have I set those with Remington? One thing our trainer always talks about is "setting the tone" with Remington, reminding him who is the leader. I have to remember that there are times that he is going to do what is expected and times he will not. If he isn't doing what is expected, why isn't he? Have I tired him out? Is he itchy and not feeling well? Is he stubborn? Is he distracted? If I don't take these factors into consideration, it is quite easy to become frustrated and short-tempered with him and others; that is when I start feeling defeated as well. I have to remind myself that it is the process, but we all know what I think of that. This puppy training is still a work in progress for me, but it is getting easier. Part of me thinks of that, saying, "Good things come to those who wait." Some days, I simply reply, "I'm still waiting."

Patience comes in other forms and challenges and is necessary when you think about the various stages of a puppy. Two particularly challenging phases are teething and adolescence. A puppy has what I call little shark teeth—sharp, little-needle teeth. They pierce things, like your skin, easily, and they will eventually fall out. During teething, they want and need to chew on everything and anything. They want to soothe the discomfort of their new teeth coming in, and they can get bitey; your ankle might serve their purpose just as well as a toy. Because of this, it is easy to get annoyed and want the dog to stop. I can tell you that I did fairly well through Remington's teething phase, with the exception of when he lost teeth. I don't do well with seeing blood, and he lost a few teeth while playing one time. There were a few times I had blood on me and wasn't sure if it was mine or his, but it was pretty cool to find the baby teeth, though.

Adolescence is its own beast, for people and canines, and I am not sure which is worse. I guess maybe it's worse for humans because it lasts longer. During canine adolescence, they are great at testing limits. If you are a parent of a teenager, this will be all too familiar knowledge. Remington is a smart dog, so it doesn't take too long for him to pick up new commands and rise to expectations. However, around eight or nine months of age, it was pretty common for Remington to "conveniently forget" what he had been taught. This was where training was also extremely helpful, as it was a good reminder that we had to reinforce to him that we were in charge, and he didn't get to just do what he wanted when he wanted.

One of the things Remington started to do during this time was to get nippy with me. On my less-than-stellar days, this would devolve into a power struggle, and then I would get angry. Actually, Remington would get angry too. Ian advised us to keep Remington off the furniture. When he was allowed on the furniture, he would see himself as at least our equal, and then he would try and assert dominance. It was a challenge to keep him off because when Remington was on the furniture, he was quiet. However, later, if something did not go his way, he would have a tantrum and get nippy. Thankfully, with redirection and reminders (more to my husband), keeping Remington at floor level worked. It really did not take too much patience on my part because I saw the results quickly. Not having bruises from Dobie nips is a plus, as is eradicating negative behavior.

Good things take time. Patience is not easy, but if we practice patience, we are really building our own emotional resiliency. While we may not realize it, we are also practicing self-compassion at the same time. We are giving ourselves a break. If you are like me and have that perfectionistic tendency or that need to control, patience helps to break those cycles.

Lesson Four: Patience

Charlie and Remington Playing

Charlie Lost His Patience

PERSEVERANCE

Patience and perseverance can go hand in hand. Where patience requires us to experience and endure challenges and difficulties without losing sight of the end goal, perseverance requires us to keep going no matter what has to be done and how long it takes.

Remington has challenged me in both qualities since day one. However, I think the concept of perseverance hit me in week two of having him home. I mentioned previously that I don't remember much of Rowdy's puppyhood. However, I do remember crying for the first two weeks of having him. During those first couple of weeks, I questioned if we made the right decision in getting a puppy. My cat of many years, GI Joe, had recently passed, and we decided it was time for a puppy. After we got Rowdy, I started to question if I was ready for another pet and if it was too soon. I was committed to Rowdy, but I wondered if I could handle the grief of losing my cat in combination with what comes with having a puppy for the first time. Also, I don't remember Rowdy's vaccination schedule with the vet being so intense either. Granted, we got Rowdy at sixteen weeks, and we got Remington at eight weeks. Rowdy didn't get any of the optional vaccinations because we weren't going to be boarding him or sending him to daycare. Rowdy only did puppy kindergarten because on graduation day, he was bitten by another dog, and my husband was traumatized by it. Sean and I were not comfortable going to another training facility, so we decided to do it all on our own.

We made a conscious decision to raise Remington differently; This meant getting all the vaccinations so he could safely be around other dogs, board, go to daycare and training. This also meant that after Remington's first vet visit, it was time to plan this out over the coming months; it meant going for a shot about every two weeks. The irony here is that now that we are a year in, at the time of this writing, those same vaccines are coming up for renewal in a month. Ahh, and there it is, that feeling of "it never ends" has crept in. I digress.

On paper, that mapped-out schedule looked good, but I didn't take into consideration that things might get postponed. They got postponed because my little guy got sick, when he had an upper respiratory infection, and that infection set back his immunization schedule. I was okay with that in theory, but in practice, I was frustrated because I wanted everything to be going according to the initial schedule we mapped out.

Once that phase was over, I was thinking I could breathe a sigh of relief. Soon after the immunization phase for Remington, we were able to start training, as I mentioned earlier. This was also when that perseverance mentality really kicked in. The issues I had with our first trainer really made me want to prove her wrong, for lack of a better way of putting it. Things like telling me he was going to be neutered early because of his behavior, and she wasn't sure we would even make it over those six months made me dig in my heels. I wasn't going to let her be right; little did I know at the time that that was going to be the least of my worries.

Dobermanns are very smart dogs, as I mentioned earlier. They need to be stimulated both physically and mentally. In my book, it is important to have a well-trained dog, but I feel it is more important with a Dobermann. So many people find them scary and intimidating. They can appear that way, but they are grossly misunderstood. If you spent even an hour in my house, you would see Remington's inner goofball out in full force. He is extremely sensitive as well.

I was happy to start training one on one with Remington because of all the reasons I have stated before, and I was really looking forward to watching him come into his own. Of course, a Dobermann coming into their own, while being an adolescent, is a challenge unto itself. While he really caught on quickly to most everything, we had setbacks, and they were not the setbacks that I expected, however. During this time period, we were starting to see some aggressive behavior of Remington toward our younger cat, Charlie. He would get very agitated and chased and growled at Charlie. We honestly thought he wanted to eat him. This was unusual because overall, both really have a great relationship together. Our trainer was the one who pointed out that Remington probably didn't feel well and was acting out.

Assuming he didn't feel well and seeing that he was itchy and had bumpy skin, we sought out help from our vet. As I discussed earlier, the vet led us down the prescription diet path; we also had a few emergency vet visits in there and a long multi-month wait to get in with the animal dermatologist. This was such a trying time for us, as we felt like so many turns took us down a dead-end path or the wrong path all together. I felt frustrated, defeated, and had more questions than answers. It was hard to be hopeful that Remington would find some relief, but we had to keep moving forward for him though.

That first visit with the dermatologist was not what we expected.

We were there for almost three hours, as the doctor was so thorough and meticulous in her exam. Thankfully, I didn't have clients until later that afternoon because I would have had to figure something out by rescheduling them. I expected to be at the dermatologist for maybe a half-hour. But when the doctor came out from the back with Remington to explain to us what was going on, we finally felt like we had some hope and some direction. She did bloodwork, a urinalysis, scoped and cleaned his ears, and completed a full allergy testing panel. The bloodwork was analyzed in house immediately, so we didn't have to wait for those results. All was well with his bloodwork, with the exception of an elevated white blood cell count, which she attributed to his ears. They were infected, and he had a lot of "goop" at the base of the ears. (I'm not the doctor here so I'm not even going to attempt to share the proper clinical diagnosis.) Apparently, the ears are widely affected when a dog has allergies. There is often inflammation in the ear canal and when that coincides with the disruption of the natural balance of yeast and bacteria, infection can occur.

We left that dermatologist appointment needing to insert and massage a liquid medication into his ears multiple times per week, and then also clean his ears on the off days of the medication. We still do this regimen, and it has made a tremendous difference in Remington's health and demeanor. We left that appointment with a grocery bag of medicines, shampoos, conditioner, gauze to clean his ears, syringes for the medication, a lot of instructions, and a hefty but worthwhile bill.

One of the things we needed to start was weekly bathing. We had two different shampoos that we needed to alternate between and a skin conditioner to use after the shampoo. Our house is set up with two full baths on the second floor and only a half-bath on the first floor. Remington was not allowed on the second floor, and it was winter, so it was too cold to wash him with the hose out back. The dermatologist also told us it was important that he be fully dried after each bath. There are special pet dryers that groomers use, which the dermatologist suggested we look into purchasing. Our groomer is great with Remington. When he was about ten weeks old, she even came to our house to give him his first nail trim outside of the breeder. I have all the necessities to do it myself, but he wasn't having any of that.

So, I asked the groomer if she would be able to fit Remington in for weekly bathing. She graciously agreed, and we started the week after I asked her. Remington only had us bathe him in the backyard with the hose, and we made it into a game to get it done. Now he had to get into a giant metal bathing station (which I had to climb into first and lure him in), and he even had to let the shampoo sit on his skin for ten minutes. Like I said, Gabby (the groomer) was (and is) great with him. She gave him a massage for the ten minutes the shampoo had to sit and reassured him the whole time he was a good boy.

Once it was time for the blow-drying, he didn't know what to expect. He was shaking and scared, jumping up and hugging me, wanting me to take him out of there. Gabby put a turban on his head to help muffle the noise. It was a process, but we all made it through, and this was to become part of our weekly routine for the near future.

Between weekly baths, weekly training, and daily ear manipulation of some sort, Remington was going through a lot. Add to all of this, we now need to go to the dermatologist monthly. Every month,

Remington needed an allergy injection of Cytopoint, and he got his ears flushed and examined each visit. While I initially was not a proponent of him getting Cytopoint injections, I do see that he benefits from them. My goal was to really address all this through holistic means and diet, but that process took a long time, and he needed relief fast.

When the dermatologist did the allergy panel, she told us it would be about six weeks before the results came back. Yes, that meant more waiting but again, we at least had a direction and felt like we were on a better path. When we went back for one of Remington's monthly visits to the dermatologist, the results were in, all eleven pages of them. He was allergic to so many things, but thankfully some of those things, like certain trees, were not native to our area. The two biggest allergens he had were ragweed and mites. His allergy to storage mites was more severe than to dust mites; this made so much sense because his worst allergy attack, if you will, was in the fall when ragweed ran rampant in our area. At that time, we obviously didn't know he was allergic, and Benadryl and other antihistamines were not cutting it.

Now that we had his list of allergens, we were at another decision-making point. We could start him on an immunotherapy regimen by either giving him a daily injection of a customized allergy serum, or daily drops that were also customized for his specific allergies. We went with the drops, as I hate needles and had to do my own self-injection once every two months because I had psoriatic arthritis. That was hard enough, so I wasn't about to inject my dog on a daily basis.

However, this is also a good example of perseverance. I have struggled with psoriatic arthritis for at least twenty years. My rheumatologist had a frank conversation with me in my mid-thirties that if I chose to ignore my condition or not take more significant measures (which at the time meant a self -injection every two weeks), I would be in so much pain that walking would be a challenge. The thought of not being active and in that much pain was not an option for me so I needed to accept that these were the cards I was dealt, so I had to self-inject a medication that was going to help me. I had to keep moving forward, and I could not give up.

Remington's allergy serum had to be manufactured out of state so it would not be ready until our next monthly visit. The drops also took anywhere from 6 to 12 months to really take effect. That was a long time, but it also puts us in decent shape for the next ragweed season. While on one level, it felt like there was a lot of waiting in this process, there continued to be hope. Hope that we were on the right path for Remington and us. Hope that the next ragweed season would be easier and more comfortable for him.

Mites are another issue. I myself am allergic to dust mites, as is my mother, so I have taken certain precautions, like encasing our mattresses, pillows, and comforters, to avoid triggering my allergies. We have had some air filters in the past, but they were not really enough. I vacuum daily but I also have someone come and clean the house on a regular basis. I should dust daily or at least weekly, but I just don't do it. I suck at dusting.

But what do you do for a dog? We did a few things. For one, his ballistic bed cover is also hypoallergenic. It is so tightly woven, he can't chew through it, and little critters like mites can't get through either. I wash all his bedding and towels in a fragrance-free laundry detergent. This is about the gentleness of the detergent, as well as keeping his area as clean as possible. I also make sure to wash his blanket the same day he gets bathed. We also bought him a Hepa filter air purifier that stays running near his crate. It is actually pretty unbelievable the amount of dust and particles that machine picks up.

Storage mites are a different challenge. Honestly, I didn't even know they were a thing until now. Storage mites are commonly found in dry dog and cat food; I guess they actually get into the food bags. There is little to no agreement on how to reduce the mites, other than to get the dry food out of the bags and put it into airtight plastic containers that are stored in a cool, dry area. I did some research, and some people will freeze their dry dog food. Some say that kills the mites; others say that there is no proof that this happens. I figured it cannot hurt, so when we get dry dog food, I immediately put about one third of the bag in Remington's airtight food container and split the other two-thirds in half in freezer bags and put them in the basement freezer, along with his raw food. He pretty much has a freezer to himself at this point.

There are so many challenges that Remington has gone through. Just when you think he has turned a corner and things are stable, something happens. He has not even been a member of this family for a year yet. At this point in my writing, he is ten days shy of a year. Remington had a decent stretch until a week ago, and then he became guarded with Gabby and with us. We knew he was uncomfortable and reached out to both the regular vet and the dermatologist for help. The dermatologist thought his experience might be better suited than the regular vet, as she didn't think it was allergy related. Not much came of the regular vet appointment, other than he tested negative for some tests, which was good, and they thought perhaps he had a soft muscle strain. We were told to keep him quiet for two weeks, which was extremely hard to keep a Dobermann quiet, especially a young one, for two weeks but we did. He was also better at the end of the two weeks.

No matter how hard the challenge is and how long it takes, remember that if you persevere, it is highly likely that your character will become stronger. Your confidence will increase, and you will be rewarded.

Lesson Five: Perseverance

Remington Determined to Make the Cat Toys His

BE IN IT
FOR THE
LONG HAUL

Being in it for the long haul and perseverance could probably all be one chapter in caring for a dog, especially one like Remington. However, I prefer to separate them out because sometime when I think of perseverance, I think of being more present and in the moment. When I think of the long haul, I think of things being more like decades out to complete. When we are in something for the long haul, we take a longer-term view of the situation, and I think there is an inherent mentality of weathering the storms with an overall bearable impact, so to speak. It's kind of like saving for your retirement. You sock money away, hopefully starting at an early age, for something you are not going to entertain dipping into for decades. You expect ups and downs in this process, and while the downs can feel scary or frustrating at times, you know you are going to come out ahead in the long run.

During our short tenure with Remington, I have had to remind myself of the long haul many, many times involving his care. In the moment, fears and frustrations can easily take over, so taking that extended view does make weathering the stormy moments more doable; it also really puts things in perspective.

When we enter into a relationship of any significance, it is a commitment, a commitment to the relationship itself, a commitment to that person, animal, job, etc., and it's a commitment to yourself. True commitment takes honesty and integrity. When we are not honest with ourselves about a situation, or we try to ignore things, it only becomes worse in the long run. When we don't have personal integrity, we essentially have nothing. Think of integrity as your true north in your moral compass. If we make decisions from a place of personal integrity, it provides consistency in our lives as well as a sense of wellbeing and reduced confusion. This allows those in a relationship with us to feel safe and know they can depend on us, as they can trust we are going to do the right thing. We won't let our true north be swayed by what others think is acceptable or popular. Think of how comforting that is. How solid that feels.

I have to remind myself that is what Remington and all of our animals need from us. They are our children, and it is our job to make sure they have safe, consistent, happy, and healthy lives: it is important that we do that to the best of our ability. In Remington's most recent dermatology visit, we learned that the bacteria from his last skin culture showed that he had a staphylococcus (aka staph) infection. The dermatologist gave him an injection of antibiotics at the last visit when she saw bacteria on the slide, and we thought we would all be set for his recovery. I even mentioned to the technician on this visit that I thought that injection really helped him. Interestingly enough, staph was resistant to what he was given; that meant Remington now needed to be on an oral antibiotic regimen for eight weeks.

Even though the technician reminded me that his skin looked so much better, I reminded her that because I see it every day and I pay attention to every minor change, panic could easily set in. I left there feeling frustrated. On one hand, I was incredibly happy to have had the bacteria narrowed down so it could be eradicated. On the other hand, I couldn't believe Remington had to be on antibiotics for eight weeks. As a side note, I hate antibiotics in general, whether they are for people or animals.

This newest discovery also meant that I needed to up my game with probiotics. Remington gets probiotics through kefir as part of his daily, healthy food routine. I felt that being on an antibiotic, it was important I added his probiotic pills back into the mix. Of course, me being me, I then needed to make sure I was prepared to help prevent him from getting staph again. I double-checked his supplements, as well as the frequency with which I was washing his bedding and bathing him. Were there any other things I should be doing? I had to really stop myself because I was going down a rabbit hole trying to help him. In that time, I had to remind myself of the big picture and long haul. I had to be objective and honest, looking at what I was doing.

The truth was I had been doing the right things, doing my best to set Remington up for a healthy life as best I could. This meant realizing too what I could control and what I couldn't. I had to remind myself I cannot keep him in that bubble. I felt for about thirty minutes that I was in this sprint for answers and prevention. Once I realized that truth, I stopped that cycle and got back to the marathon.

If we think about the long haul in situations in life, there are some practical tenets that need to be in place. One example is to pace yourself. It's easy to want things right away or in a relatively brief period of time. The more we advance technologically, the more we have at our immediate disposal, and we don't have to wait. We can literally Google anything and have immediate answers instantly. Something happens in the world, and we get instantaneous notifications, so there really isn't much down time. So, the long haul forces us to delay gratification and sometimes put things on hold.

In my opinion, one of the things that helps in pacing yourself is to chunk things down. When I say chunking things down, I mean breaking tasks, projects, or ideas into smaller pieces. For example, if I have a day of back-to-back clients, I think of all the aspects that go into that day. Before I even get to the office, I make sure that I have prepared all my snacks and meals for the day; that way, all I have to do is throw them into my lunch bag before I leave in the morning. On my way to work, I prioritize what I need to do in order to be present for each person. For me, this means pulling everyone's charts as soon as I get in, reviewing the last session and making sure all I have to do when they leave is write the session notes. This offers me a foundation from which to start, and I don't feel like I have tasks hanging over my head before ending my day.

Back-to-back client days can be overwhelming and intense. Sometimes I find it helpful to even just take my day one hour or one session at a time. It feels much more manageable to do that instead of thinking I am in sessions from 9 a.m. to 7 p.m. with no break. Having smaller, more manageable goals each day serves a few purposes: it keeps us on track; it keeps us moving forward, but it also provides a sense of accomplishment. It can be easy to lose sight of the end goal or even feel like it will never happen. Having steps in place reminds you of where you are going. Even those smaller goals need to be realistic in terms of time frame as well, whether for yourself or for your pet. Are you setting daily, weekly, and monthly goals? If you are a casual runner and your pace is a ten-minute mile, it isn't realistic to think that next week, you will hit an eight-minute mile. However, it may be realistic to think of shaving off some amount of time in the next few weeks and months.

This brings me to discipline, which is a big one and a subject to which I know I will not do justice. People draft whole books just on discipline. The bottom line with discipline is that with it, we take the goals and plans we have outlined and reap the rewards of the end results, which are accomplishments. Discipline can really be a formidable challenge. To remain disciplined, it may require us to make decisions that are not popular, not what others expect or want from us; it may also take time away from entertainment or social events and so on for us. It really requires us to know ourselves, as we need to know what our strengths and weaknesses are. We all have them, but we need to be honest with ourselves about them. Some people have weaknesses regarding certain situations or with other people. Others have issues with food, alcohol, or budgeting. Some don't have healthy coping strategies when it comes to difficult or emotional circumstances. Whatever yours is, you need to factor that into a long-haul plan.

The same goes for your strengths. What are your strengths, and how can you maximize them? Are you a good organizer? Are you a strong strategist? Are you a people-person and charismatic? Is it easy for you to ask for help and employ those around you for support and encouragement? Whatever your strengths are, use them to work smarter, not harder.

Sometimes our strengths and weaknesses can be one. As an example, I am an empath, and I feel everything. Ask my parents; I cry at the drop of a hat. I feel intensely, and this is both a strength and a weakness. Feeling intensely can be exhausting, where it can skew my decision-making and perspective. I have to consciously take a breath, regroup, and ground myself during intense moments. I often need time alone to recharge and recover. (Yes, clear introvert right there too.) However, being an empath is also a strength, allowing me to authentically sit and be present with my clients. It allows me to connect with them and identify (but not overly so and not without boundaries) in ways that they feel comfortable and keep moving forward in their own work. Sometimes I complain that I feel like I have a neon sign above my head that says, "Please talk to me and tell me everything!" It drives me nuts when I am in a waiting room for my own appointments, and the person next to me starts telling me their life story unsolicited. I apparently give off some vibe that makes me approachable in certain situations, but I have to embrace that because it is also what allows me to be good at what I do professionally.

When I think of my strengths and weaknesses regarding Remington, I have to remember that he has them too. He has qualities that are inherent to his breed, and he is unique unto himself. What might seem like a silly example is that one of his strengths is that Remington is a fast runner. Dobermans can run up to thirty-five miles per hour. I love that he can run fast; it is amazing and beautiful to watch, and it makes playing frisbee fun. I also have to remember that because he is a fast runner, I am not going to beat him. I am not going to get to that frisbee before him, and I sure as hell better try to get out of the way if we are on a collision course for one another. For the longest time, I would try and scoop that frisbee up before he could. Unfortunately, I had the bruises to prove it, so now I realize that it is just not a part of the game worth engaging in on my end.

I also have to remember with Remington, his weaknesses or challenges mean more training needs to happen on my end. If he is anxious or sensitive in certain situations, I have to work with him to make those situations more tolerable and in smaller increments. If he is counter-surfing and didn't get caught, that means he most likely got rewarded, and now I need to up my game with training to correct that unwanted behavior. Is that unwanted behavior going to happen overnight? It is highly unlikely, and we are no different. We can't expect to wake up tomorrow, and our patterns will be different. However, again, if we are aware, we can make changes that last.

This is where discipline comes into play. How many people do you know (this might even be you) start something, are gung-ho about it, and then, after a few weeks, are right back where they started? After that, they may even be more frustrated or disappointed because they took a step back. Discipline is demanding work, requiring commitment and focus. It's also important to understand ourselves to know what kind of discipline we respond to. Are you the kind of person who responds well to constructive criticism or corrective measures, or do you respond better to supportive discipline, which is going to help you either stay on or get back on track? Are you setting yourself up for success by making sure that you have preventative discipline in place?

In thinking of myself, especially in relation to raising Remington, I respond best to supportive and preventative discipline. I am able to respond well to corrective measures from an external source; if they are presented in the right way, I trust that person and respect them. In the past, if I was challenged in a provocative or public manner (as by our first dog trainer), I would not respond well and become either angry or defiant. When that happened, I had to take some time to process my own emotions before I could rationally think about what was being presented to me; this was so I could then reframe what information I was just given. Only then could I decide if that information worked for me and the ultimate goals that we had for Remington or not.

When I think of supportive discipline, one of the first thoughts that comes into my mind is one's natural support system: that can be our family, our spouse, our friends, or our coworkers. When you think of these people, are you surrounding yourself with the right people? Do the people in your life support you? Do they encourage you and have your back? Are they honest and candid with you, even when it might be difficult? If they give you feedback, can you hear it from them and accept it?

When you have people in your life who are supportive, it enables you to stay on course or right your course if you have strayed. They help you to become the best version of yourself. If you think about it, usually when we have surrounded ourselves with good people who support us, we also feel more confident and secure, which is important when you are doing things that require long-term perspective.

It is easy to get caught up in the trees and lose sight of the forest. That is why some people need a plan, which brings us to another type of discipline: preventative discipline. This might sound strange because you might think, *What am I trying to prevent?* As an example, I have had to use preventative discipline in authoring this book. I haven't been rigid about writing it, but I have done things like removing distractions when I write. I know what times of the day all my animals are quiet and will allow me to sit with my thoughts. Also, I try and set expectations for myself. Even when I don't really feel like writing, I try to write something so that I keep the momentum going.

Does that mean I write daily? No. It does mean that I do expect to take no longer than a two-week break in between writing sessions. Ideally, I would write daily, but I work and have responsibilities that

I have to tend to as well. Quite frankly, sometimes I have zero desire to write, and I have given myself permission to not force it if that is the case.

When I started to write this book, I wrote a lot. Almost daily and in manageable chunks. I did that partially to prove to myself that I was going to keep at it, and it felt important to set that tone for myself. I also have the expectation of myself that when I sit down to write, I am going to write until the desire, or the words, stop. I have had to make concessions as well when my fingers start to jam up from my arthritis. At times, I have given myself a break, while at other times, I stopped all together, and both have been okay to do. I've had to remind myself this is a marathon, not a sprint. It is going to take time, and how much time, I don't know.

Remington's trainer's facility is stark so there are so few distractions for the dogs. It is literally a room with two chairs, which we would sit in, a place for Ian to sit and when we worked on place with Remington, a bed for him to sit or lie on while training. The starkness allowed Remington to focus solely on what we were working on. Ian would provide distractions once our dog started to master a skill. We would always joke that Remington was the perfect student, and he did great at school. But when he got home, it would be a different story. It is hard to remove distractions in our house when we have three other animals inside and then two chickens outside. We also have people who walk and run down the street, some with their own dogs and have cars and delivery trucks that frequent our road. While we have a long driveway, the dogs can still see all of this, and both want to protect their property.

With Remington, I had to find ways to reduce his distractions. One strategy I have is to take him into the backyard. The chickens are back there, but we are lucky that he doesn't chase them or even want to play with them for that matter. When the resident turkey or deer stroll through, that is a different matter. Then both dogs go into "get out of my yard" mode. In the backyard, I found that I could keep Remington relatively focused, where I could switch between play and disciplined commands, and it was easier for him to learn from me. It wasn't the simplicity of his formal training environment, but it worked well enough to have the things we were working on come through at home.

Inside the house was also a different story. Even today, I have to be disciplined when working with Remington inside. With Rowdy and Charlie (our orange cat) often wanting to be in the mix, I need to control what variables I can during Remington's training. I have to work on preventing Rowdy from distracting Remington when it's bedtime. Remington doesn't want to always go into his crate at bedtime. If Rowdy is downstairs, getting Remington in can be particularly challenging, and he will be stubborn or bolt out of his crate toward Rowdy. If Rowdy is upstairs, it is much easier.

It also is a pattern, not always but enough that we have to pay attention to it, where Remington will get the zoomies or be amped up about fifteen minutes before bedtime. When he gets the zoomies, all of the area rugs go flying. He throws himself up on the couch and then back down, and it doesn't matter if someone is on the couch or not. Rowdy might feel trapped in one spot, and then he starts to bark. It's a circus. Again, when that happens, we have to work on calming Remington down enough to get him into bed and to listen. If we let that just go on, chances are one or both dogs could get hurt. Sometimes it is admittedly hilarious to watch, but the key is knowing when enough is enough for everyone involved.

Discipline is tough. There are days and times when you just don't care or want to put forth the effort, and that is a normal feeling. But if you cave into that lack of discipline, especially if it becomes a pattern, you are setting yourself up in the worst position to fail, but at the least, you will encounter a roadblock or lose your momentum that you have probably worked hard to achieve. I think of this in relation to Remington, and one of the things that comes to mind is being disciplined regarding repetition. Humans and canines need to be repetitive in order for something to take hold in their minds. If we consistently do things over and over, they become habits and develop muscle memory. Our body and mind say, "Oh yeah, I remember this."

I remind myself daily how important it is to review the basics with Remington. He has known sit, stay, down, etc., for a long time, but it is built into his routine on a daily basis. That repetitive reinforcement comes through in clutch situations. When I think of clutch situations, I think of circumstances that may put Remington, myself, or others in a precarious or dangerous position. For example, I have dropped things on the floor that if Remington ate, it could make him sick. My reinforcing the "Leave It" command has mitigated that risk.

Just the other day, a neighbor was walking her dog and was at the end of the driveway. Both dogs saw them, and Remington started running down the driveway toward them while barking. As soon as I instructed him to "Come," he stopped, turned around, and came back. Had we not worked on that and continued to do so, the outcome could have been different, and that neighbor could have been frightened.

This is where, in my opinion, goal-setting is important. If we develop long-range targets, that will help us keep our eyes on the prize, so to speak, and our end goal will remain in sight. The key to getting there will depend on our short-term goals. When I think back to training with Ian, our overall goal was to have a well-mannered dog. We knew people would judge him based on his breed, so it was important for us to have him obey commands. Every training session we had goals, and then we had things to work on between that session and the next. Sometimes these felt like leaps and bounds, and other times, they felt like we took a step backward. The steps backward were often related to his skin and allergies, which impacted how Remington felt. When he had bad allergy weeks, our homework was low-key and sometimes simply reviewing what we had learned. Sometimes during those weeks, it was ridiculously hard to maintain my perspective to be hopeful. I wondered if we were ever going to take the next step.

Probably the biggest hurdle Remington (and I) had to overcome was his pulling on the leash. I don't mean just pulling but being good on the leash and then full force darting into a run. When he did this, I would have to let go; otherwise, I would get dragged. We are not that far off in weight, and he is a hell of a lot stronger than I am. I was inadvertently also showing him that it was okay to do what he was doing. There were a couple of weeks that the only thing we needed to work on was the corrections for when Remington would do this on walks. I vacillate between "Ugh, this is never going to work, and I am going to give up on the leash. Every time he does it, I will just let go," and "We've got this, buddy!"

That first line of thinking was seriously flawed for many reasons. Mostly, it was defeatist and didn't take into consideration his safety and that of someone or something else. I didn't spend a lot of time with those thoughts, but they were there, and I needed to pull myself out and reframe my thinking on more than one occasion. We still have to work on this with Remington, but he is so much better. I am also better at catching and correcting him, and he responds accordingly. It can still be an issue though. When he is super excited to see someone, I have to really be prepared and brace for the pull and correction. We are not at perfection, but we certainly have made progress.

One of the many things I appreciated about our training time with Ian was his clarity. We always knew what the goals were and what we needed to do. Having clear goals again keeps you on track and on the right track. In the therapy world, if you accept insurance, insurance companies are big on measurable goals. They want to know exactly what you are doing and how you are doing it. They want to see that the client is making progress and what they are paying for is "working." That isn't always easy, and there is a subjective component to all of it. However, again with clarity, everyone can be on the same page.

As I have said, discipline is difficult. It can feel like a grind on you, so it is important to incorporate and practice self-care into your day and week to reset. You do what you can do, even if only for five minutes a day. When some people hear the words self-care, they think it is a selfish act, thinking it is wrong to prioritize themselves. We all know intellectually that we can't be there for others if we are not taking care of ourselves. Then why is it so hard for us to do self-care? There are so many reasons for that, but I will not even get into it here; that could be its own book.

Think about it though. If you are burned out and have no reserves, your patience is probably low, making it hard to concentrate or solve problems. You may not feel joy or excitement. You might also be in survival mode and are going through the motions as best as you can. I liken it to a good night's sleep; when we get enough rest, we are refreshed and can embrace the day. When we are running on a few hours of sleep, we may push through, but it is just that—a push. It's one foot in front of the other. There is no exuberance, so the day generally runs smoother when we get adequate sleep.

Being in it for the long haul is the same. Yes, we are going to have bad days, but we have to make time for ourselves. I can tell you that when Remington was little, I had many days that felt like I was at my wit's end. Between him, the other animals, the house, and work, I was whooped. My daily self-care practices slowly (some rather quickly) went out the window, and everyone paid for that. It wasn't just me. I was short with my husband. I had no tolerance for things like routine emails and phone calls. Because I was so taxed, anything that disrupted my day or, in my mind, what my day should look like resulted in me being frustrated or in tears. That is no way to live.

I do have to do this periodically, but before, I had to take note of the things that were part of my self-care regimen that had fallen by the wayside. Once I had that itemized in my head, it was time to get back to implementing them again. Some of these were things that literally took a minute. For example, I often start my day setting my intention for the day. It could be something like, "Today, I am going to stay calm," or "Today, I am going to be mindful of what I do have (rather than what I don't have)." It is amazing how something so simple can set you up for success in your day. I needed to bring those self-care practices back into play to feel more grounded, to be present for my husband, my animals, and my clients.

Self-care looks different for everyone, coming in different forms and from different perspectives. I think of self-care from the physical, emotional, spiritual, and even financial viewpoints. You may have other ideas or things you want or need to nourish and pay attention to. Keeping all these pieces of the pie in order and healthy again keeps us in the marathon. I'm not expecting or asking anyone, or myself, to be perfect, but I am asking you and myself to be realistic and balance life to the best of our abilities to develop long-range targets that are achievable.

Thinking long-term can be challenging. It might feel like the ultimate goal is too far off, or there are too many steps necessary in achieving that goal. Breaking things down into manageable pieces and being disciplined will get you where you want or need to go. Have faith in yourself and your process.

Lesson Six: Be In It for the Long Haul

Remington Looking Over His Golf Course

YOU ARE GOING TO FUCK UP

One of the things that comes up a lot in therapy with clients is parenting issues. So many parents worry that they are going to mess their kids up, not set them up for success, or otherwise do them unintentional harm. Well, guess what, you probably will. It will also probably not be as bad as you think.

I didn't want and don't have kids. Well, not human kids. My animals are my kids, and that fear of doing things wrong, or, in my words, fucking up was very real. My parents have a cottage on their property that they would rent. When I was in high school, my parents took in a Doberman that was abandoned by one of their tenants. She was such a sweet girl, but her previous owner really did fuck up. She came to us full of problems that never had to happen. The Doberman had a lot of different worms and who knows what she had been exposed to. We gladly took her in and got her ship shape in no time. She became a great dog.

Somewhere along the way, she had some good training. I don't remember her ever being on a leash, as she knew her commands and was overall a quiet but formidable presence. Whatever neglect she had been through in her past life seemed like ancient history after she became part of our family.

When it was time to consider another dog, I was torn between a rescue and breeder. There are so many animals out there that need good homes and until we adopted our Maine Coons, all my animals have been rescues. I've wanted a Doberman for a long time, and I was fine with a rescue but was also worried about what that would look like with three other animals who were well established in the house. Starting with a puppy seemed like the best option, so a reputable breeder it was.

When you start with a puppy, you have a clean slate, which in some ways feels even more intimidating. What you teach them and expose them to is really on you. Our breeder did an excellent job starting from the time they were born introducing new things. Previously, I spoke about socializing and having a list of all the things I wanted Remington to be exposed to. It was a bit overwhelming for me to think of accomplishing all of that in an abbreviated period of time. One of the mistakes I think I made was really trying hard to check all the boxes for his experiences. I literally was checking boxes and crossing things off the list. What I wasn't paying attention to was if I was overwhelming him with all these tasks and stimulation.

Hindsight is 20/20, and there is that saying about if I knew then what I know now. I had people telling me to take it slow and enjoy bonding with my puppy. I was also keeping track of developmental stages and trying to do what I was "supposed to do" during each stage. If I am honest and look at my mistakes now, here is what I think I did. I think I overwhelmed Remington. I think I overstimulated him, putting him in situations that he was excited about but probably were not the healthiest for him, given his immune system and burgeoning skin issues. I put him in doggy daycare, which exacerbated his skin issues and itchiness. Now looking back, I'm not sure if I asserted my dominance in the best ways either before I was shown how to properly exhibit leadership with him. I had many days that I became easily frustrated and yelled at him, telling him I was going to give him away. I mean the list goes on.

If I were beating myself up, I would say, "Wow, you fucked up in a major way!" Did I make mistakes? Of course. Did I ruin my dog and traumatize him forever? Absolutely not.

When I think back to those examples, there is a part of me that laughs, a part of me that is astounded, a part of me that feels terrible, but most importantly, there is a little voice inside of my head that reminds me that I did the best I could do.

Reflecting back to when I brought Remington to Tractor Supply, he was excited to be there, and it was probably a lot. When he was older, I took him there again to check out the washing station, and I had a new attitude. I knew he would be highly stimulated; it was essentially an unfamiliar environment, and he was bigger and stronger. Though I was better prepared, it was still kind of a shit show. He pulled me around, even on his prong collar, smelling all the smells and trying to take home all the treats and food in those aisles. It was a short trip, but I was definitely more prepared, and I also knew that would be a lot for us both, so we had to do something fun when we got home.

The doggy daycare issue is hard because it would be so nice for Remington to be able to spend the day away so I could get things done, but it is not healthy for him. Most professionals that I have encountered are not proponents of doggy daycare. However, I understand why they exist and why people need and like to use them. For Remington, that was not the best option, as it was not worth the risk to his health. I remember him coming home thinking he had so much fun, and he was over-tired. That must be why he was wriggling around on his back and growling. Nope! It took me a fair amount of time to put together that the other dogs, whether it was getting scratched while playing, playing in the pool and coming home wet, or simply being exposed to a lot of dogs that may have had some underlying conditions, were not healthy for Remington. Not healthy to the point that if I look back at it, he very well could have developed his warts from all that exposure.

I also think that Remington was probably getting mixed messages from a training perspective. He definitely tested his limits there, and I know that he scared some people. It was easy to look at Remington and think he was an adult dog because of his size. The other piece is that the daycare did have structure to their day, which I liked, but it had to be confusing for Remington. We had a very regimented structure at home, and it was not the same. Again, he was young, the daycare option was helpful for us, and I thought I was doing the right thing. Thinking on it, it probably was a blessing that he got kicked out.

I knew from the jump that I was going to have to assert my dominance with Remington for many reasons. One thing that I started doing early was pinning him to let him know I was alpha. When I told our trainer Ian, he laughed at me. Thankfully, I wasn't the first to tell him that, but he showed me alternative ways to show I was the alpha. We knew that it would be necessary, especially when he became close to outweighing me.

When Remington started adolescence, his skin issues really started to develop too, so it was a very trying time for all of us. I was easily overwhelmed and frustrated during that time and had days where I would yell to try and get him to do what I wanted him to do, which usually meant I really wanted him to stop a certain behavior, such as biting or jumping. I am not going to lie; there was a time that his behavior made me nervous and anxious. I felt he was unpredictable, and that made me feel a loss of control. Screaming at him was not effective or helpful. When clients tell me they yell or raise their voice, I remind them that the person at the receiving end will often shut down or tune you out when you are doing that. No one likes to be yelled at, and we really don't respond well to it.

The message you are trying to impart is utterly lost at that moment. I intellectually knew that, but my amygdala took over, and I wasn't rational. Because of this, I felt embarrassed too because I knew the neighbors probably heard me, and I knew what I was doing was not going to give me the result I desired from Remington. Also, let me tell you, I can't speak for all Dobermans, but Remington does not respond well to being yelled at; he either gets mad too or puts his ears back and is confused.

One of the things I talk about with clients a lot is being human, making mistakes, and trying to accept this truth. When we make mistakes and fuck up, hopefully, we learn from it. Learning from our mistakes requires reflection, humility, and a willingness to take risks. It means we have to be willing to do things differently and try things that may make us uncomfortable. I know those feelings all too well. That being said, had I not been willing to make changes and try new things with Remington, I would still be stuck on a hamster wheel and probably have a very untrained, poorly behaved dog.

Part of what I am talking about too is the concept of embracing failure. You are probably reading this and saying to yourself, "What the hell is she talking about, and why would she even want to put that out there?" Well, the truth is we are going to fail. We aren't just going to make a mistake, but we will fail somewhere along the line.

Your failure could be a relatively small failure, or it could be significant. However, failure can also be the catalyst for growth. To even think of failure requires some level of bravery, risk-taking, and knowing in the end you will be okay.

The power of positive thinking is real and important when thinking about failure, which I weave into my sessions with clients every day. I think we also have to be realistic as well. Life isn't all rainbows and fairy tales; the sooner we realize failure is part of the equation of life, the sooner we can continue to move forward and live more fully.

Not one of us is perfect. Accept that you have flaws, are going to make mistakes, and that the world is not going to end because of that one misstep.

Lesson Seven: You Are Going to Fuck Up

Remington Looking Fabulous In His Custom Fleece

CONFIDENCE IS KEY

Someone told me the other day that I carry myself with an air of authority and knowledge, which is why people always come up to me, ask me questions, or think I work at places that I don't. I laughed when I heard that because, as I shared earlier, I often say I think I have a neon sign above my head that says, "Tell me your life story!" It works well for me in my profession but drives me nuts when I am on my own time. The person then reframed it to one word, which is "confidence."

Confidence is something many people struggle with. This might be because some people have received messages over time that they are not enough, told through a critical parent, teacher, boss, or someone in authority. Poor academic or work performance can lead to a lack of confidence. Failed relationships or financial stressors can lead to a lack of self-confidence. Confidence is about your ability to be sure of yourself. You are secure in knowing you can handle something or that you are a good person. You know your strengths and limitations, and you know what you are capable of.

For the most part, I have always been a confident person, in some areas more than others. Have I had my weak moments? Absolutely. Even when those weak or challenging moments happen, I do know deep down in my core that everything will be okay. However, sometimes accessing it can be another story.

Remington has really tested my confidence as a pet parent and a leader. I have mentioned before that our dog trainer Ian always stressed leadership and confidence. He could tell when I wasn't confident in our training and about the lesson he was suggesting. I was honest when reporting back to him about what I felt was working and what wasn't in our training at home. Some of the time, I had to give it time. Ian would often tell me to do training exercises in short stints. Ironically, this was for both Remington and me, as those short bursts allowed me to build my confidence in how I was presenting myself to Remington, and it showed him that I was serious and meant business. When I wasn't confident, it ran right down that leash, and he could tell so Remington would take advantage of that too.

Ian would tell me that Remington could sense when I wasn't confident as well. It could be in the way I carried myself in my posture and gait, or in my tone. I think this is a good point to make in terms of confidence. The way we carry ourselves says a lot about us. I remember when I moved to Boston to attend my undergraduate studies, I was in a completely new environment. To go from living in a small town to a city was a jump. It was fun, but it also didn't take two months for me to have my wallet stolen right out of my handbag in the middle of the day; that forced me to be more aware of my person and my belongings. In my mind, that also meant I had to look like I belonged comfortably in town and present myself with assuredness. Presenting myself with assuredness is something I have done the majority of my life but being conscious of it as an adult is a different level of awareness.

When you have those weak moments as an adult, you can remind yourself that you can turn things around and, as cheesy as the phrase is, you can fake it till you make it. On the surface, if you do it enough, it really works, and you aren't faking confidence anymore. There are other steps to making confidence settle in and truly take root though.

Some of the things that contribute to confidence-building are concepts I have mentioned in other sections of this book. I cannot stress enough the power of positive thinking. Our mind is such a powerhouse, and we use only a fraction of it. Why not harness what we can?

What does it mean to practice positive thinking? I like to think of the power of positive thinking from a two-pronged approach. There is the internal, mental dialogue part, and there is the somatic observation and feeling part. The mental dialogue part includes the things you say to yourself. Are you filling your mind with self-criticism, or are you building yourself up? Some people think that mentally building yourself up feels silly. Telling yourself you love yourself, you are a good person, you are a smart person, and the like might feel strange. However, the more you do it, the more you will embody it and believe it.

If you are repeating positive affirmations and envisioning success for yourself, you are increasing the possibility of grounding yourself, along with being open to feeling your emotions. When we are in a negative headspace, it is easy to feel less confident, defeated, or incapable. When we are focusing on something with a positive mindset, we are also being intentional and present; this allows us to then move over into the somatic realm. If we are paying attention to our thoughts, especially if we are replacing negative thoughts or "old tapes" with positive thoughts, we have the opportunity to be aware of what our bodies are experiencing. For example, when we are "happy," we often feel "light" or a sense of freedom. When we are sad, angry, or are in a negative headspace, we might feel "heavy," burdened, or sluggish. That plays out in our bodies as well. If we are feeling down, we may not have motivation or enthusiasm, whereas if we are in a positive space, we feel like we have drive, confidence, and the ability to enjoy and be present.

Positive thinking does not happen overnight, as it takes practice. One strategy that I have found effective is to combat the negative self-talk or thoughts by essentially talking back at them. For example, if your inner dialogue is saying something like, "I am so stupid! I can't believe I did that!" you can combat that with something like, "I am no stupid. I am smart." If you made a mistake, it's important to tell yourself, "It's okay. I made a mistake." "I am human." "It is not the end of the world." Am I oversimplifying? To an extent, yes, but you get the gist. It's about turning the negative statement into a positive.

There is a caveat to positive thinking that is worth mentioning. Just like anything, we have to be careful of extremes. It is possible to be too optimistic. If you are positive at the cost of minimizing the gravity, difficulty, or reality of a situation, this can be harmful. It is important to maintain a balance and be grounded in reality. If something terrible happens, it is necessary to acknowledge this and not minimize it. Being overly positive in that situation may create barriers to not just your processing and growth but your relationship with others.

Confidence and positivity go hand in hand in many ways. If you think of it, when we are confident, there is a certain ease we can bring to the table. But how do we foster and maintain this confidence and positivity? Again, let's be realistic. You are going to have your bad days, and you won't feel great a hundred percent of the time.

As we have discussed before, it's important to surround ourselves with a positive and supportive network of people. That can be family, friends, and colleagues, but it also extends to our social media and screen activity. Listening to uplifting and success-oriented podcasts can be helpful. Being part of groups that promote growth and success can be rewarding. People and posts that make you think and elicit a sense of curiosity and wonder are beneficial.

Some of the most confident people are able to see the different facets of a situation, disagreement, opinion, etc., and are okay with the differences. In fact, they are open to the differences; this is actually true of being a Doberman owner. Dobermans have been portrayed as vicious, scary dogs. When I tell people that we have a Doberman, I am usually greeted with a myriad of responses. Some love it and think they are great dogs. They especially love it when they meet him and see how friendly he can be. Some people automatically get wide-eyed and are fearful. They don't want to come to the house and think he is going to hurt them or attack them. Is he large, protective, and intimidating? Yes, he is and can be. He is also a huge goofball, and we lovingly refer to him as a level four cling-on. People do judge me for his breed. If I cared, I probably never would have gotten him, but I would also be missing out on a great dog. We didn't make the decision to get Remington based on what other people thought but on what we wanted.

My husband and I have also had a lot of challenges with him, for which I think other people would have rehomed him at that point. There were definitely times I was not confident that things would be okay with Remington; this came up the most around his allergies. When we were getting hit by one thing after another, it was exceedingly difficult to be positive and not be all doom and gloom. Almost a year after starting Remington's process with the dermatologist, I am truly confident that he is on the right track. His skin is so much better than a year ago. His attitude is better because he feels better. Personally, I can look to his future and legitimately know that we and Remington are going to be okay and can face what challenges come our way.

Having that year now under our belt has also given me the ability to reflect and take stock. I can look back and give myself and my husband credit for what we have done: that means Remington's healthcare, his training, and his socialization. It means giving myself credit for not giving up. It is important to celebrate our wins and successes; oftentimes, if we don't do it ourselves, it won't happen. Yet we look to others to make that happen.

Do we need validation in our lives? Absolutely. Do we need support and constructive feedback? Yes. However, we cannot solely rely on outside commentary or influence for our confidence. The most significant source of strength, confidence, and self-esteem need to come from within. That can feel like a tall order, but it is possible with work and consistency.

It is necessary that we treat ourselves and others with respect. When we or someone else do not have a lot of self-confidence or self-esteem, being harsh or mean isn't productive. More often than not, we will treat ourselves worse than we treat others. This is a surefire way to chip away at your self-confidence. How many of you have those old, negative tapes playing over and over in your head? How many of you have standards for yourself (but not necessarily others) that are unrealistic and unattainable? It can be challenging to set realistic expectations for us but when we do, we will find success comes more easily.

I saw this with Remington when I set the bar at a realistic level. More often than not, he meets my expectations but also exceeds them.

It's time we treat ourselves with the expectations we have of others. We will be pleasantly surprised. The more we do this, the more personal wins we will experience and the more we can celebrate. Celebrating our successes and achievements is not being conceited; it shows us that we really are enough and, in most cases, have worked hard to earn those celebrations.

Practice positive thinking and positive self-talk and make choices based on what is best for you. Walk with your head held high, knowing that it is more than okay to be yourself in this world.

Lesson Eight: Confidence is Key

Remington's Confidence On Display

YOU DON'T ALWAYS GET WHAT YOU WANT

When we thought about getting a puppy again, I conveniently forgot the challenges associated with a young puppy. It had been twelve years since we got Rowdy, and my memory seemed to focus more on the funny mishaps, the harmless mischief, and just how cute Rowdy was when he was little. The excitement that led up to Remington was palpable. We had waited a long time for him, and I had my own ideas of how things were going to go and progress. That idealized side of me was excited for the cute, rambunctious pup that was going to fit in perfectly with our family. The realistic part of me knew it would be a lot of work and a significant commitment to time, training, and overall adjustment.

Despite that realism, idealism took over without me knowing it; that is probably why I spent money on Pendleton beds that Remington just eventually tore up. I bought blankets and toys that lasted a hot second. I thought he would miraculously listen because he is smart.

I wanted an easy, seamless transition with our new dog. The transitions with the other animals weren't seamless but in hindsight, they did go well overall. The person who had the hardest time was me. As you know, I talked about this throughout this short tome, using countless examples from my animals.

To cut to the chase, it was hard for me to accept that I didn't get what I wanted. I had gotten used to the energy level of a senior dog. I had gotten used to only three animals in the house, and only one requiring being out in the cold to do their business. All of them, with the exception of Charlie, did not have health issues that took months to figure out. For the most part, things were straightforward. There have been very few things about Remington that are straightforward. However, I do think we are finally getting to a place where we know him well enough so that we can predict or at least expect certain responses and behaviors from him.

Remington's first year plus was so unpredictable. From trying to figure out if he had food allergies and what was going on with his skin to his staph infection and getting a parasite, it just felt like it was never-ending, and we didn't get a break. Just when I felt like things were coming under control, we would get hit with something else. It was hard because his behavior wasn't predictable either. Yes, he had the traditional puppy life stages that he went through, but his other trials made it hard to enjoy his development and youth. We have since learned that everything really depended on how he was feeling.

This idea of not getting what you want I think everyone handles it differently. Some people handle it with grace, while others pitch a fit. Remington is currently in the adolescent phase, so he is all about pitching a fit. You take away something he isn't supposed to have, and he pitches a fit. You have to leave the lake, and he's not ready to go. He pitches a fit. It's time to come inside, and he's not ready, so he pitches a fit. You see the trend here. I like to think I am more evolved than Remington. Not all days this feels accurate, but that being said, if I started to see this same pattern in myself, I would have to ask the question, "What do I need to do to get through this? What will be helpful, constructive, and hopefully less explosive than the type of barking and nipping fit Remington engages in?"

Not getting what we want can bring up a myriad of different feelings. For example, anger, frustration, disappointment, confusion, despair, sadness, anxiety, or self-esteem issues. The intensity of these feelings can be in direct proportion to what you didn't get. The intensity can also be blown out of proportion if it feels like the hits keep coming and everything is compounding. I think it is important to allow yourself to feel whatever is coming up. It might not be an opportune time to do so and if it's not, make sure you make time later on. So many times, people stuff down how they feel and ignore it. Then, when something else happens, these feelings are triggered; they come back up and get displaced where they shouldn't be. It can be hard to sit with your feelings in general, especially when you don't get what you want. No one wants to feel crappy and sit with the yuck. However, if you sit with the yuck, you can move through it and move on.

Acknowledging your feelings about not getting what you wanted can lead to feeling like a failure, an embarrassment, or even make you feel "less than." Now that you have identified how you feel, what do you do with that? There are a lot of things you can do. Talk to people. Tell people what has happened and how you are feeling. When Remington was in the worst of his undiagnosed allergies and multiple random skin issues, I relied a lot on my friend Erin, who I mentioned earlier. I needed to tell someone how frustrated I was. How scared I was for him. How angry I was. I wanted that easy, fun puppy, and what I had in the worst moments was a grumpy, itchy, uncomfortable, and reactive puppy. I felt like nothing I was doing was working and felt sad for him and for us. I was tired and scared that things would never change, and his life would forever be an enormous challenge. See any black-and-white, fatalistic thinking going on here?

At times I felt like a bad pet parent and even a bad wife. My thoughts were consumed by Remington, and I didn't feel like I had room for much else. I didn't even try to write a journal because I didn't have the wherewithal. This was because I was so focused on finding solutions for him, as well as feeling incredible anxiety, that coping skills were tough to come by. It felt more like survival.

However, as things slowly fell into place, and I mean slowly, I was able to take a step back and was more grounded. I didn't know it at the time, but I did start utilizing other skills and strategies to deal with my disappointment. The fear started to subside as well, which helped to acknowledge that there was a lot of fear for Remington's situation and how we were going to navigate it. I reminded myself that in the end, everything works out the way it is supposed to.

Saying out loud that Remington's puppyhood was not what I had expected or wanted allowed me to start moving through everything more effectively. I had validation from others. I was able to change my thinking to be more optimistic. I was able to reduce my attachment to the outcome. At some point, I realized that I had become overly attached to Remington's struggles, and not his successes. How awful is that? Success rarely happens when focusing on the negative, so changing that focus from negative to positive made a world of difference. It helped me realize that I may not have gotten what I wanted in a puppy, but I got what I was supposed to have.

Even working through that idea wasn't easy. We all want things to be fun and easy. The real reward, as corny as it sounds, is in the work. The work, the effort to move through feelings and change the mindset, makes it possible to achieve acceptance and put the disappointment behind you.

In some situations, you might feel like you are going through a grieving process, which is something I went through. I grieved the loss of the puppyhood experience I wanted with Remington and had hoped for. I grieved the perception of that perfect Doberman pup. In truth, I had a velociraptor who was challenging, difficult, and infuriating. He was also hilarious, goofy, curious, and entertaining: that describes Remington to this day. The bond he and I have is complicated and sweet.

The bottom line is that we may not always get what we want, but the universe has a funny way of giving us what we need. It is not necessarily an easy road from the start of that sentence to the end but therein does lie the truth. You may have to employ multiple strategies and support systems to get through the process, but it's possible and important to do so. Pitching a fit like an adolescent Doberman is not the answer. Acting like a mature adult, who can honor their feelings and disappointment, comes from a place of strength and growth. It is something to be proud of.

Do we grieve the loss of what we hoped for? Absolutely. However, when we shift our perspective, we can see that it's okay things didn't turn out as we imagined. Sometimes what we receive is even greater than what we expected. Stay open to the possibilities and opportunities that are unfolding before you.

Lesson Nine: You Don't Always Get What You Want

Remington Getting Just What He Needs—To Run

BE GRATEFUL AND HAVE FUN

There is one last lesson to share, and it is on gratitude. Gratitude is powerful and can literally be life-changing. We can be grateful on both small and large scales. People tend to think of gratitude in terms of the massive things. For example, having a lovely home to live in, having graduated and received a degree, being able to access quality care or resources: these are all valid and real. Personally, one of the biggest things I am grateful for is my health. When you are healthy and take care of yourself the best you can, no one can take that away from you, and at least, for me, it is empowering.

Expressing gratitude is also particularly important on a smaller scale. This is often where I start with clients when they feel they don't have important things to be grateful for. When I think of smaller-scale gratitude, I can go really small. Small things can include being grateful for the taste of that yummy cup of morning coffee. It can be the fact that you got out of bed before noon, or that you got dressed today. Some people would disagree with me on that example, but if you are someone who is struggling with severe depression, which can be a very real thing, it would be important to acknowledge that as progress.

When I relate gratitude to Remington, a lot of things come up in my mind. I can say that depending on the day, it depends on my level of gratitude. Right now, as I am typing, he is booping my hands as I try and type. While it is driving me nuts, I am grateful that this boy brings me joy and fun. However, there have been many days when I struggled around gratitude and really did have to look for the small things. At this point, he seems to be in a bit of a calmer, happier place. His allergies seem to be well-managed, and he is starting to mature a bit. Remington still pitches his fits and gets mouthy when he gets caught doing something he isn't supposed to do. That being said, he is also pretty hilarious when he is being fresh. My husband might disagree with that one, especially when it's his stuff he is running around the house with and won't drop. The funny part is when he starts prancing with a sock or shoe insole in his mouth because he is being ignored. He seems to think the more regal he looks, the more acceptable his transgression will be.

On a bigger scale, I am grateful for Remington's loyalty and protection. I know that I am always safe when he is with me. I am grateful that he does well with people, and people that interact with him love him. I'm grateful that he keeps me active and engaged, especially on those cold winter days when I would rather stay inside where it is warm. I'm grateful that he pushed my limits in ways that I did not anticipate or expect, as he has shown me different sides of my character. I acknowledge some parts I do love and others not so much. However, I appreciate the attachment we have to one another and the challenges and rewards that it brings.

There are a lot of benefits to practicing gratitude: these include things such as improved health, improved relationships, and enhanced emotional flexibility. Earlier, I talked about gratitude on a small scale and on a large scale. I think of the smaller scale items as building blocks for the larger-scale items. For example, if I am grateful for having healthy food, clean water to drink, clean, and cook with, it makes it easier for me to see the bigger picture of being grateful for my overall well-being and health. When I am able to do that, I also feel happier and have a more positive outlook.

When we practice gratitude, we actually have some biological functions that kick in. That feeling of happiness that I talked about is a direct result of the production of neurotransmitters dopamine and serotonin; these are the "feel good" chemicals that our brain produces. The more we engage in gratitude, the greater the likelihood of having a positive attitude and feeling rewarded.

Gratitude can also decrease anxiety and depression, helping to reduce stress overall. Our prefrontal cortex becomes engaged when we employ gratitude practices, and this part of our brain is responsible for emotional regulation. This is also where our working memory, planning and goal-setting ability, and decision-making ability are located. When our executive functioning center is activated in a positive way, we are able to improve our cognitive functioning. We feel in control, grounded, and mentally flexible, and these things are directly correlated to improved mood and decreased anxiety.

Another way that gratitude practices help to reduce stress and anxiety is through the reduction of cortisol. Cortisol is a stress hormone and when we have too much of it, we can feel anxious or depressed. Studies have shown that daily gratitude has shown to reduce cortisol levels upwards of approximately 20% (MPH, 2020). When we feel less stressed, anxious, or depressed, it allows us to be more present in our relationships. We have the ability then to improve our social bonds, and when we feel better, we are more likely to want to help or be generous with others. We are more positive and thus most likely pleasant to be around. As people, we enjoy being with people, and they, in turn, enjoy being with us. One of the big problems that people experience is loneliness, so gratitude can help combat that in both small and big ways.

Think of how you feel when someone compliments you or holds the door open for you. Some people will say they are embarrassed or feel rushed when witnessing this, but my experience is that at the root of all of that is being thankful. They are thankful that someone took the time to comment on something they liked or took the time to notice you had a big, bulky package and could use the door being held open.

How do you express gratitude? Do you take action, or are you verbal? Do you express gratitude differently in your internal world than you do when you are engaging with the external world? Do you wait for the perfect moment, or do you act in the moment?

When showing genuine appreciation, why put it off? It sounds corny, but the reality is that life is short, and we are not guaranteed the next moment. So, if you want to tell someone or show someone that you appreciate them, why wait? Say how you feel. Show them how you feel. Let that person or group share in that dopamine rush you are having because you are thankful. Leave that note in your kid's lunchbox telling them to have a wonderful day and that you love them. Bring your coworker a coffee just because you appreciate them. Take your neighbors' UPS packages out of the rain so they don't get ruined. Give yourself a pat on the back because you are the only you that you have.

Give that Doberman the best life you can, because he is giving you his life and his unconditional love.

Cultivating a practice of gratitude has immeasurable benefits for you and others. It grounds us in the present moment and gives us hope for the next day.

Lesson Ten: Be Grateful and Have Fun

Sarah and Remington at the Golf Course

REFERENCES

Clinic, Cleveland. *How to be Patient: 6 strategies to help you keep your cool*. Cleveland Clinic. June 5, 2024, https://health.clevelandclinic.org/how-to-be-patient

Clinic, Mayo. *How to stop negative self-talk*. (n.d.). Mayo Clinic. Accessed on November 7, 2025. https://www.mayoclinic.org/healthy-lifestyle/stress-management/in-depth/positive-thinking/art-20043950

Davis, Tchiki. PhD. "6 Ways to Boost Self-Discipline: Figure out your 'why.'" *Psychology Today*. December 3, 2023, https://www.psychologytoday.com/us/blog/click-here-for-happiness/202209/6-tips-to-boost-self-discipline?msockid=366a15a67fde669e1d5f01e57e9d6726

Developing your classroom management plan. (n.d.). Columbia University. Accessed on November 7, 2025. https://www1.columbia.edu/sec/dlc/dkv/cero/0511/index_bin/0511_s0_eval.html

Fds, J. W. *The Doberman Pinscher: A complete breed overview*. Doberman Planet. December 30, 2021. https://www.dobermanplanet.com/doberman-pinscher-breed-overview/

Fds, J. W. *How to Choose Which Type of Doberman to Get (with Examples)*. Doberman Planet. September 16, 2022. https://www.dobermanplanet.com/what-doberman-should-i-get/

Gleeson, B. "9 Powerful ways to Cultivate Extreme Self-Discipline." Forbes Magazine. August 25, 2020. https://www.forbes.com/sites/brentgleeson/2020/08/25/8-powerful-ways-to-cultivate-extreme-self-discipline/

National Archives, *Let the Records Bark!* National Archives. May 5, 2023. https://www.archives.gov/publications/prologue/2011/winter/marine-dogs.html

MPH, N. K. "How practicing gratitude is a key coping strategy for feeling less stress." *Psychology Today.* July 7, 2020. https://www.psychologytoday.com/us/blog/comfort-gratitude/202007/gratitude-helps-minimize-feelings-stress?msockid=366a15a67fde669e1d5f01e57e9d6726

Ortiz, M. The 1st Marine War Dog Platoon were the 'goodest bois' of WWII. *We Are the Mighty.* May 28, 2021. https://www.wearethemighty.com/articles/the-1st-marine-war-dog-platoon-were-the-goodest-bois-of-wwii/

Student Behaviour Management, *Preventative, supportive or corrective discipline?* Student Behaviour Management. May 3, 2016. https://studentbehaviourmanagement.wordpress.com/preventative-supportive-or-corrective-discipline/

Putney, W. W. *Always faithful: A Memoir of the Marine Dogs of WWII.* Simon and Schuster, New York 2002

Rhp. Wounded combat dog during action on the Orote peninsula, 1944. *Rare Historical Photos.* September 14, 2025. https://rarehistoricalphotos.com/wounded-combat-dog-1944/

Staff, E. P. *23 Ways to Increase your Self-Confidence.* Explore Psychology. July 23, 2025. https://www.explorepsychology.com/self-confidence/

Team, G. *How to be More Patient: 25 Tips for Increasing Patience in All Parts of Life.* Goodwall Blog. November 12, 2024. https://www.goodwall.io/blog/how-to-be-more-patient/

Utiaitsaccts. *War Dog Background.* College of Veterinary Medicine. May 18, 2023. https://vetmed.tennessee.edu/about/war-dog-memorial/wardog-background/

ACKNOWLEDGMENTS

First, I would like to thank my parents, William and Donna Benoit. They have supported all my endeavors and adventures. Since I was young, they have encouraged me and supported my efforts in whatever path I chose. They challenged me and were the voice of reason when I was not so reasonable. They have always encouraged my creativity, whether it be through my writing, my love of music, my business, or my self-expression. I would not have come as far as I had without their support. Remington and I are both grateful that we are fortunate enough to spend time with you at the lake. I am happy that you have gotten to see Remington, and probably me, grow as he continues to go through his velociraptor phase. Thank you, and I love you, Mom and Dad.

To my husband, Sean Keating: Boy, do you put up with a lot from me. Thank you for bearing with me on my hairbrained ideas and my substantial endeavors. Thank you for being by my side through the fun parts of life and the really difficult parts of life. The fact that you did not divorce me during Remington's puppyhood is a testament to your fortitude. While Remington has brought us joy and fun, he has also challenged us as individuals, as a couple, and as a family. I think Lucy and Rowdy will forever have a little part of them that says, "What were you two thinking?" Sean, you are my stable rock, my unwavering support, and for that, I am grateful. Thank you for being the best hubby ever! I love you.

To my friend Erin Flanagan, who helped get me through some of the most unpredictable phases of Remington's young life. The education you have given me, the resources you have shared with me have been so valuable. I will never forget the crate schedule; that helped me so much. When I felt like I was unraveling and was rampantly texting you, you did not brush me off, and you did not waiver. You understood and continue to understand. Not only do you validate me, but you give me suggestions that help me solve problems. Dobies are a special breed, and Remington appreciates that his Auntie Erin has his back.

I cannot thank our trainer, Ian Martin of Absolute K9 Solutions, enough. Ian, your knowledge and methods were perfect matches for us. You took a wholistic view and made me think about things I otherwise may not have given much thought to. Your observation of the changes Remington went through were not only helpful but also affirming. Your patience with him, especially when he was not feeling well, was extremely helpful. Thank you for helping me break things down and giving me permission to slow things down, so that I could come into a place of leadership with Remington. I may never be the true alpha, but I'm pretty damn close.

To everyone who has contributed to Remington's development, has supported my journey with him, and has supported the writing this of this book, thank you.

ABOUT THE AUTHOR

Sarah C. Benoit is a licensed psychotherapist in New Hampshire, Massachusetts, and Maine, with over twenty years of experience. Her private practice is based out of Milford, New Hampshire, and she specializes in trauma recovery.

Mental health is Sarah's second career. She started out in business after graduating from Northeastern University with a Bachelor of Science degree in Business Administration. After five years in the business world, she went back to school and pursued her Master of Science in Counseling Psychology from Fitchburg State University. Since then, she has actively pursued her career in mental health. During the pandemic, she wanted to expand her knowledge and completed a certificate program in Plant Medicine at Cornell University. In addition to working directly with clients, Sarah is also involved with podcasting, which you can learn more about by going directly to her website, www.sarahcbenoit.com.

Sarah currently lives in New Hampshire with her husband, Sean Keating, their dogs, Rowdy and Remington, their two cats, Lucy and Charlie, and their six chickens. Sarah enjoys spending time on the water, spending time on the coast of Maine, and having adventures with her friends and family.

It was important to Sarah that she authored this book because she was pleasantly surprised how during Remington's puppy stage, she had to rely on the professional advice she shared with clients on a daily basis. She knew she was not alone in what she was experiencing and wanted to offer strategies to others in the hopes that they would make their puppyhood journey easier.